Eat Like A Lady

Guide For
Overcoming Bulimia

Carla Wills-Brandon

Health Communications, Inc.
Deerfield Beach, Florida

Carla Wills-Brandon
Clear Lake City, Texas

Library of Congress Cataloging-in-Publication Data

Wills-Brandon, Carla
   Eat like a lady.

   1. Bulimia. I. Title.
RC552.B84W55   1989   616.85'2   88-24551
ISBN 1-55874-008-2

©1989 Carla Wills-Brandon

ISBN 1-55874-008-2

Publisher: Health Communications, Inc.
        3201 S.W. 15th Street
        Deerfield Beach, Florida 33442

Cover design by Vicki Sarasohn

Dedication

This book is dedicated to:

My husband Michael, who is my partner
and dearest companion on this journey called life.
My son Aaron, who unknowingly continues to teach
me about myself and the world in which we live.

Contents

Acknowledgments

As a result of being in my own personal growth process, I have had the opportunity to meet and share with a number of people whom I consider to be guides and mentors. I have crossed paths with those whose influence has been through personal therapy, recovery programs, books, workshops and more. There also have been many courageous individuals who have trusted enough to share their pain with me while struggling toward peace of mind and recovery from addiction. In addition, there are the family members whose influence continues to affect me in ways that bring great joy and, on occasion, pain, while providing motivation for my own personal growth process.

I believe life is full of teachers, but for the most part, very few of them are aware of how they have affected my thoughts, views and perceptions about life. There are many whose influence has surfaced both directly and indirectly within this book. I thank all from the bottom of my heart, but would like to specifically acknowledge those I feel made the book possible.

First I would like to express my appreciation to Pia Mellody for her work with shame, abuse issues and the recovery process. Many of her concepts of shame are intertwined in this venture. Along with her, I would like to thank Elisabeth Kübler-Ross for her work with grief and the grief process. Her work in this area has had an impact on my life both personally and professionally. I would also like to express my appreciation to Janet Woititz for her working with adult children of alcoholics and defining the rules and traditions within those family systems.

There are also those who are directly responsible for making this book a reality. I would like to acknowledge and give a special thanks to Rita Baker, who waded through and typed pages of handwritten material that now lives within the pages of this book. Only those of us who type with one finger can fully appreciate the work Rita has done. My appreciation goes to David Cross for initially reading through the first part of this work and providing suggestions and directions. David also is responsible for the exercise section in the book he urged me to write.

I would like to thank Marie Stilkind for her support, encouragement and direction, which allowed me to have faith in this project. Last but not least, I would like to thank my husband, Michael, who not only helped me with the title of the book, but also provided constant encouragement and support during its preparation.

PART

1

The Disease Of Bulimia

1

How It All Started: A Personal Journey

Hello, my name is Carla and I am a recovering alcoholic, drug addict and bulimic. I decided to put this short book together for several reasons.

Personal Recovery

First of all, when I finally made it into recovery for my alcoholism and drug addiction, my bulimia began to escalate and I had nowhere to turn. I was experiencing more pain and confusion than before recovery and would sink into feelings of loneliness, uniqueness and *shame* every time I attempted to discuss my problems with food. My family and friends would be shocked, confused and concerned when I described my pattern of *binging* (unrestrained eating) and *purging*. I went to several therapists who appeared to have difficulty addressing my bulimia as a result of lack of information and education. I began realizing that the shame I would feel in response to the reactions of others seemed to precede my eating binges, and eventually I would find myself back into denial about the seriousness of my eating disorder. Several times I wondered if recovery was really all it was "cracked up to be" and considered giving up. But, I didn't give up and I did find many answers. Now I want to share that part of my life of which I previously was so ashamed.

Hope And Support Available For Bulimics

My second reason for writing this is to let the individual, who has already identified himself or herself as bulimic, know that there is hope and support available. Initially I did find a great deal of support from those who are addicted to white flour and white sugar, but I still felt unique in that I would binge on celery, lettuce or apples and would use raw green beans as a natural laxative. Those who didn't understand at all would say, "Carla, you stopped your chemical usage, so stop your bulimia the same way." The idea sounded simply wonderful, but the doing seemed impossible.

In time, I found many individuals — some already in one form of recovery or another for chemical addictions, co-dependent addiction, work addiction, etc. — who were experiencing or previously had experienced the pain and shame of bulimia. They shared their feelings of frustration around the inability to eat in a healthy manner, and many would share their pain about being able to put down the booze, pills, joint, line, relationship, etc., but not the five candy bars or entire bag of chips and dip. During this time I began to realize that food had been a problem for me for a long, long time. While I was growing up, I would hear "eat like a lady," but I had no idea of what friends and family members were talking about. Eventually recovery from my eating disorder became possible. This didn't occur all at once but slowly through trial and error and self-examination with the help of workshops, recovery programs, concerned therapists and the love of friends and family. It is possible for us to find a solution to bulimia.

Bulimia: Misconceptions And Myths

My third reason for addressing this issue is to give some information to the reader who is curious about his or her own eating patterns and is undecided as to whether the behavior is bulimic or not. I have listened to a number of misconceptions and myths about what bulimia is and have seen these myths perpetuate the disease. For example, several years ago I was watching a television program on bulimia. During the program a bulimic woman ate an entire cake with her hands while sitting on the floor making animal noises. I felt sad and disappointed with this portrayal of my disease and became even more distressed when I overheard a group of people discussing the program several days later with the understanding that this was what bulimia was all about. I never ate an entire cake (let alone on the floor with my hands), but I am a bulimic and my disease almost killed me. A myth existed that said all alcoholics were skid row bums, and I believe this misconception kept a number of functional or closet alcoholics from recovery. Similarly, I believe that because of limited public and professional awareness about the disease of bulimia, many bulimics are remaining in denial about the seriousness of their illness and are not seeking help. Regardless of the misconceptions and myths, I discovered that there were some truths about my disease. *Bulimia is chronic, progressive and can be fatal.* Recovery is necessary for growth. I discovered I was going to have to take small steps, ease up on myself, explore who I was, feel my feelings, slowly become my own best friend and make a commitment to my own recovery. The impossible did become possible.

2

What Is Bulimia?
Denial And Delusion

You might be asking what exactly bulimia is and what some symptoms are that seem to appear on a consistent basis. Many bulimics seem to have an inappropriate concept of their body shape and size. For example, while in my disease if I was weight appropriate or less, I usually felt a need to reduce by ten or so pounds. Some bulimics who are overweight may be in denial about just how overweight they are. At one point in my disease I was very overweight but could not picture in my mind's eye what my body looked like realistically. I would delude myself into thinking that I was smaller than I really was.

Quick Test For Bulimia

Try this quick test to see how in tune you are with yourself. Close your eyes, and in your mind's eye try to picture what your face and body look like. Now go to the mirror and look closely at yourself. In your mind's eye could you picture your face accurately? Did your mind's perception of your body at all match what you saw in the mirror? For years I had so much shame that I couldn't even see my face in my mind's eye. When I could picture my body, it was very distorted. This is an explanation of bulimia that I have found works for me. If you have more information to add or a definition that suits you, by all means use it if it provides clarity to your concept of the disease of bulimia.

Disguises And Consequences Of Bulimia

Denial is at the base of all addictive disorders, and bulimia is no exception. Depending on the form of bulimia, the denial can wear a number of disguises.

Binging And Vomiting

For the bulimic who is binging and then vomiting, it is difficult to deny that there is a problem because the consequences are obvious. For the recovering alcoholic or addict, vomiting can no longer be attributed to excessive chemical usage and hangover. But *rationalization and minimization* tell oneself, "I'll wait 'till next year to work on it," or "It really doesn't hurt me that much."

Many of us used alcohol, drugs, relationships, work, sex or other addictions to cover up our feelings. As we get into recovery for those issues, feelings begin to surface. Purging through vomiting puts a halt to the recovery process because the shame of this disease perpetuates the cycle of binging and purging that can cover up the feelings vitally necessary for growth. Vomiting can be mood altering in that one may experience light-headedness, fatigue, numbness of mind, depression and a variety of mood swings. These altered states make it difficult to truly experience feelings in a healthy manner and resolve issues. Our feelings about what is going on around us become distorted, and the problems of everyday life seem overwhelming.

Medical Consequences

There also are a number of medical consequences to purging through vomiting. Some of the possible physical consequences are rupturing the esophagus or stomach; experiencing heart palpitations; hormonal imbalance and menorrhea; decreasing potassium level (along with a loss of other minerals and nutrients necessary for a healthy body) and damaging the teeth. Purging through vomiting can create consequences that are irreparable. An extreme example is of a recent autopsy report on a young woman that cited the cause of death as bulimia with purging by vomiting.

Laxative Abuse

Laxative abuse as a form of purging appears to be much easier to rationalize in comparison to vomiting. This form of purging can consist of over-the-counter laxative products in the form of pills, candy, gums or tonics. There are also many natural laxatives such as raw green beans, health food products and prune juice. Some bulimics use enemas as a form of purging. Denial for this type of purging can take the following forms: "I've always had bowel trouble," or "If I don't, I feel constipated." Laxative abuse can adversely affect and even damage the natural process of elimination to a point where one truly is physically incapable of having a bowel movement without the use of laxatives. Other consequences may involve a loss of essential body fluids and nutrients and, in severe cases, damage to the gastrointestinal tract and rectum. Recovery often involves time to allow the natural process of elimination to return.

Exercise Abuse

Exercise bulimia is probably the most elusive of the purging methods because it is disguised as "healthy." Exercise can become a way of burning calories to justify binging behavior. A healthy exercise program is just that, healthy versus obsessive. Aerobics seven days a week or daily visits to the gym may be forms of bulimia in disguise. When I talk to someone who is extremely upset about missing one day of exercise out of a rigid weekly program of jogging, swimming, racquet ball or any other type of exercise, I begin to suspect a possible eating disorder in the form of exercise bulimia. Despite a medical doctor's recommendation, some individuals will continue their exercise program. They will do so too soon after surgery, in spite of an injured joint or before having fully recovered from a physical illness like the flu. Consequences can involve further physical injury or illness and an avoidance of feelings as a result of obsessing on the exercising activity.

Anorexic Bulimia

Another type of purging behavior is in the form of *anorexic bulimia.* This involves a period of fasting or abstaining from food intake followed by binging behavior, for example, "I didn't have breakfast or lunch so I deserve a big dinner."

There are also those who could be termed periodic "bingers" who may adhere to a strict diet for periods of time with intermittent lapses in binging behavior. The individual who only allows himself a health food diet but then finds himself binging on tacos and pie one afternoon may be practicing a form of bulimia. In addition, there are those who binge on large quantities of health foods and feel their behavior is justified because the food is "good for you" and that makes it acceptable. If one sits down and eats a very large bunch of celery and carrots in a short period of time, one is still binging.

Basically, it gets down to how we are using food to cover up what is really going on in our lives. What feelings do we need to be feeling (instead of eating 10 sugar-free popsicles or a bag of cookies)? What is our shame really about? Are we angry or do we hurt? What loss are we trying to fill? The eating behavior is a symptom and a cover for a much larger dilemma. To begin with, we might want to ask ourselves, "Who am I and why am I so scared?"

3

Fear, Feelings And Facing Reality

While in my disease of bulimia, I wasn't aware that my eating disorder was a symptom of something much larger. What I was aware of were my feelings of terror about gaining weight and being out of control. I knew that I had used chemicals and relationships to avoid my feelings about myself and began to wonder if possibly that was what caused my bulimia. I remember watching other people eat and wondering, "How can they do that?" There were times when I thought that I would never get to the bottom of my bulimia and that I would be forever trapped in my mental prison of obsessive behavior around food, my weight and body appearance.

Vicious Cycle Of Bulimia

The disease of bulimia can become a vicious cycle beginning with feeling pain, anger, shame and even inflated joy. These are culminated by covering up the feelings with binging and purging.

Recently a great deal of information has been published on the disease of co-dependency. The concept of co-dependency came as a result of working with family members of chemically dependent persons. Counselors, therapists and others involved with chemical dependency treatment began to notice a specific set of similar behaviors in a majority of family members and discovered that these individuals were usually just as dysfunctional as the chemically dependent persons. These individuals avoided their own issues by trying to fix or take care of the chemically dependent person. This not only kept the chemically dependent person from suffering the consequences of chemical usage, but also kept the family members out of touch with who they were individually. Eventually, family therapists and others working with dysfunctional family systems, where alcohol or drugs were not the issue, began to see that the families they were involved with had characteristics similar to the families affected with chemical dependency. Thus, the concept of co-dependency came into being.

An easy definition of co-dependency is that it is an inability for one to experience a healthy relationship with self, others or a Higher Power as a result of not knowing how to communicate honestly, feel feelings and trust. It appears that the disease of co-dependency runs in family systems from one generation to the next (like the disease of chemical dependency) and continues until the cycle is broken with recovery.

There are a number of wonderful books which discuss this topic in depth, such as: *Co-Dependent No More* by Melody Beattie, *Co-Dependency — Misunderstood, Mistreated* by A. Schaef, and *Lost In The Shuffle, The Co-dependent Reality* by R. Subby. At this time, our attention will be focused on the disease of co-dependency as it relates to bulimia.

One of the core issues for the disease of co-dependency appears to be the overwhelming feeling of shame. The type of shame we will be discussing appears to be the basis for most addictions and their perpetuations. Shame, in small doses, is necessary because it reminds us that we are human, are not perfect and can make mistakes. It suggests that we are not the center of the universe and that we live in a world with many others. An example of healthy shame might involve a situation in which one discovered the zipper on her dress wasn't zipped up all the way.

Rarely do we know we are experiencing unhealthy shame when the feeling arises. Usually when it becomes apparent, we believe we are experiencing guilt. Shame also can be disguised as feelings of uniqueness, inner isolation, incompetence, emptiness, hopelessness, inadequacy or aloneness. When experiencing an overdose of unhealthy shame, one feels like a mistake or a defective human. One doesn't see oneself as a whole human being. One feels one is missing something that everyone else seems to have. When making a mistake, instead of learning, growing and forgiving oneself, one becomes the mistake.

Co-dependent Behavior

Many bulimics talk about the shame spiral, which is the feeling of sinking deeper into shame. Usually this experience appears to be preceded by a number of behaviors. The following is a list of co-dependent behaviors taken from an introductory reading for Co-dependents Anonymous (CoDA) meetings. This recovery program is based on the 12 Steps of Alcoholics Anonymous (AA), with a similar meeting format. The list specifies particular behaviors that cause difficulties for individuals in relationships with others, with self and, in many cases, with a Higher Spiritual Power or concept.

1. My good feelings about who I am stem from being liked by you.
2. My good feelings about who I am stem from receiving approval from you.
3. Your struggle affects my serenity. My mental attention focuses on solving your problems or relieving your pain.
4. My mental attention is focused on pleasing you.
5. My mental attention is focused on protecting you.
6. My mental attention is focused on manipulating you (to do it my way).
7. My self-esteem is bolstered by solving your problems.
8. My self-esteem is bolstered by relieving your pain.
9. My own hobbies and interests are put aside. My time is spent sharing your interests and hobbies.
10. Your clothing and personal appearance are dictated by my desires as I feel you are a reflection of me.
11. Your behavior is dictated by my desires as I feel you are a reflection of me.
12. I am not aware of how I feel; I am aware of how you feel.
13. I am not aware of what I want; I ask what you want. I am not aware; I assume.
14. The dreams I have for my future are linked to you.
15. My fear of rejection determines what I say or do.
16. My fear of your anger determines what I say or do.
17. I use giving as a way of feeling safe in our relationship.
18. My social circle diminishes as I involve myself with you.
19. I put my values aside in order to connect with you.
20. I value your opinion and way of doing things more than my own.
21. The quality of my life is in relation to the quality of yours.

Many repeat co-dependent behavior over and over, despite the consequences, because of a lack of awareness about choice. This is not the way it is supposed to be.

The one characteristic that keeps a number of individuals from recovery for bulimia is the inability to ask for help. Usually on the outside a bulimic appears in control, attractive, healthy and successful. Bulimics can be the world's greatest listeners and problem solvers, and they rarely say no. The word "no" was completely foreign to me, and I had to learn to use it for my own recovery. When a bulimic goes into a shame spiral, it is usually not for public viewing. To a bulimic asking for help seems impossible. When I asked for help, I would experience even more shame because there was a part of me that believed I wasn't worth it. This is called being in a *shame-bind.*

Many have grown up in family systems where it was not acceptable to ask for help. Statements like "Be a man," "Pull yourself together," "Stop being a cry baby," or "Do it yourself and be a big girl," are responsible for creating adults who have difficulty asking for help. At times, it appears easier to withdraw emotionally than to ask for help. The feeling of shame, which can result from reaching out to others, can seem overwhelming. A bulimic can appear in control on the outside and at the same time be trapped in shame on the inside.

There were times when on the outside I appeared very confident and at ease with myself, while on the inside I was sinking deeper into a shame spiral, fearing it would be discovered that I wasn't confident or at ease with myself. For many bulimics, because the shame-bind involves asking for help, it is not possible to move through the issues associated with the feelings of anger, pain, sadness, aloneness and fear. Instead, they are covered up with the binging and purging cycle and rarely resolved fully.

Illustration Of Binging And Purging Cycle

To break the shame cycle, it is necessary to begin to feel all feelings, including shame, without covering up with binging and purging. We need to realize that our feelings will not destroy us and that we can pass through them, finally resolving those issues related to them. It is almost impossible to resolve underlying issues without a willingness to begin addressing bulimic behavior. Other matters of concern are being able to ask for help and allowing others to be supportive in spite of the shame-bind.

In order to begin recovery, it was necessary for me to realize that my bulimia was a tool I had developed in order to survive painful situations in the past. This survival technique had been my best friend and comfort for years, but it was preventing me from discovering who I was. I began to see how my survival tool was backfiring and was needing to be replaced with healthy tools. It was time to ask for help and become a whole human being. In order to begin changing some of this old behavior, it became necessary to take a look at where the bulimia had originated and why it was initially so essential for survival. See Figure 3.1.

Figure 3.1. The Shame Cycle*

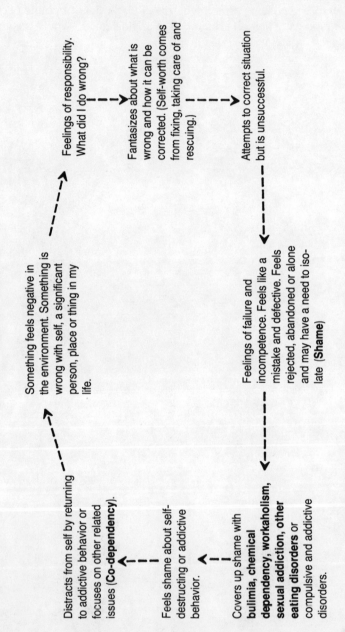

Something feels negative in the environment. Something is wrong with self, a significant person, place or thing in my life.

Feelings of responsibility. What did I do wrong?

Fantasizes about what is wrong and how it can be corrected. (Self-worth comes from fixing, taking care of and rescuing.)

Attempts to correct situation but is unsuccessful.

Feelings of failure and incompetence. Feels like a mistake and defective. Feels rejected, abandoned or alone and may have a need to isolate (**Shame**)

Covers up shame with **bulimia, chemical dependency, workaholism, sexual addiction, other eating disorders** or compulsive and addictive disorders.

Feels shame about self-destructing or addictive behavior.

Distracts from self by returning to addictive behavior or focuses on other related issues (**Co-dependency**).

* Involvement in the Shame Cycle also is about inappropriate or nonexistent communication skills plus a tendency to overreact, to be hypersensitive and to feel overly responsible and fearful.

4

Survival: How The Disease Of Bulimia Originates

When I reached recovery for my bulimia, I began to realize that I had a difficult time understanding what my feelings were. I felt like I was raw, and for the majority of that time during early recovery my feelings were very intense. For years I had covered them up with one form of addiction or another. In recovery I was finally able to begin the process of sorting out who I was and what fears I had been avoiding. At times, the pain would feel overwhelming, but I was grateful just the same that finally I could feel true, pure and unclouded feelings.

In a dysfunctional family where there is alcoholism, drug addiction, eating addiction, workaholism, sexual addiction, gambling addiction or any other addictive disorder, the members of the family develop a number of defense mechanisms and survival techniques on an unconscious level that make it possible for them to live in the system.

For example, if a 10-year-old girl lives in a family where Dad is a rageaholic and throws things when he gets angry, the young girl will

17

probably develop a number of behaviors that enable her to survive in this home. She probably knows with 95 percent accuracy when Dad is about to rage and what precautions she needs to take to feel safer. It may involve hiding in the closet, emotionally detaching by reading fairy tales, or it may be that she eats so as not to have to feel the rage or tension in her home.

When this young girl grows into an adult woman, she will take with her from childhood her survival skills that enabled her to survive with rageaholism. She may find herself in situations similar to those she grew up in, but her survival technique may not be effective anymore. Many of us from dysfunctional families are still using survival techniques from childhood in our present day lives. These techniques may no longer be functional. What they do is keep us from knowing ourselves.

The disease of bulimia is a survival technique, which many of us developed at some time in our lives. Some may have discovered it early or later in life, finding it useful to deal with the many unspoken feelings of fear, loneliness and shame that were not safe to share. We also may have discovered that even though our family situation was chaotic, we could control what our bodies looked like. We began to realize that there were ways to control how we appeared to the rest of the world on the outside. I always thought that if I was acceptable on the outside, maybe I would begin to feel acceptable on the inside. To be in control gave many of us a false sense of security by keeping us from feeling the pain around us.

I realized that this false sense of self kept me walled away from who I really was. If the wall began to crack, the feelings of pain, shame and fear could quickly be covered by bulimia. I believe that my bulimia was my best friend for many years. But eventually the friend that once kept me safe and insulated began to turn on me, and I was trapped in a way of life that was void of any hope for growth. The shame of the addiction perpetuates the addictive behavior.

Some bulimics develop other addictions, such as alcoholism, drug addiction, workaholism and sexual addiction, as a means of covering up the shame associated with bulimic behavior. I found that with alcohol I could control my bulimia and feelings about my bulimic behavior. In time I lost control over my alcohol usage and became addicted not only to food, but also to alcohol. Others may have found bulimia while already in another addiction. For example, the sex addict who experiences shame as a result of promiscuous behavior may find that binging and purging is effective in covering up feelings of unworthiness. Still others may put down one addiction and pick up bulimia. For example, an alcoholic may achieve sobriety and recovery for alcoholism but find that food is now becoming a problem. Switching one addiction for another is called *cross-addiction*. As long as we fear our feelings we will continue to cover them up.

Most bulimics and other addicted individuals come from families where there are three unspoken rules. These rules are also developed on an unconscious level and were the rules our parents, grandparents and great-grandparents grew up with. These rules perpetuate the cycle of shame that can make us vulnerable to addiction and its continuation.

Don't Talk About What Is Really Going On

This first unspoken rule is exemplified by a father who is caught up in his work addiction; the entire family is aware of it, but it isn't discussed. Mom may be angry and hurt but tells her children everything is all right. When unresolved issues in a family are not discussed, they will be acted out by the members of that family. In this sample family, the older daughter may be throwing up after every meal, and other children in the system may be fighting. Everyone is aware that there are a number of problems in the family, but nobody feels safe enough to talk about it.

The attitude in a dysfunctional family is that if it is ignored, it will resolve itself. I have seen seriously anorectic bulimics continue to live in their disease while the entire family denies that there is a problem. To the outside observer, the dysfunction in a family may be very clear; but for the family in denial, reality is not visible. If it is not discussed, it does not have to be explored. For those who are aware that there is a problem, there still may be some resistance to addressing the dysfunction, such as "I know I'm bulimic, but if I talk about it, I will hurt and probably have to change."

Certain Feelings Are Not Acceptable

In this second family rule, feelings are the enemy, especially feelings of anger, sadness, shame, guilt and pain. Some may even fear that their feelings will either become overwhelming and out of control or that feelings will kill them. If a small child grows up in a family where Mom loses control and rages every time she is angry, the child may grow into an adult who fears his own anger and the anger of others. When he does feel anger, he will probably try to cover it up or ignore it. I believe human beings were given feelings for a reason; if we do not process how we feel about what is going on around us with our feelings, they will come out in a dysfunctional manner. Getting angry does not mean losing control and raging. Research is beginning to find that a large number of physical illnesses are related to an inability to process feelings and deal effectively with the stress that is created by not listening to how we feel.

While involved in my addictive diseases, the primary feelings I attempted to avoid were anger and shame. I had a fear that my anger would overpower me, and my shame would destroy me.

In a healthy family, all feelings are accepted and validated. If a young girl comes home from school crying and hurt after being tripped on the playground, it is very appropriate for her to feel her feelings for as long as she needs to do so. If she is told to be a big girl and stop crying, she will not be able to heal. Instead, she may carry the pain with her. It may not be appropriate for her to trip the child who tripped her, but it is healthy for her to experience her feelings.

If we are allowed to feel our feelings, we can pass through them and learn from the experience in the process. If we are denied our feelings, they will eventually come out in some form that may not be appropriate. As a bulimic I was not able to process my feelings, and in turn I was not able to grow and move on. Each time I was confronted with a painful situation, I would avoid it with addiction. My bulimia and obsession with food, calories and weight distanced me from my own pain temporarily. Bulimia also kept me from dealing with feelings of anger, shame, unworthiness and fear. While in an addiction, it can appear to be less painful to obsess on the addiction than to face who we really are, but this is an illusion. Most of us fear we will not like who we find if we give up the addiction. Some of us fear there will be nothing there.

Don't Trust — The World Is Not A Safe Place

This third rule means many have an extremely difficult time with trust because it is not acceptable to talk about what is really going on around us or to experience all our feelings in a dysfunctional family. We find it difficult to trust ourselves, others and sometimes even a Higher Spiritual Power. Children learn how to trust themselves and the life process by feeling safe and trusting the environment they grow up in, as well as those adults who are a part of it.

For example, if Mom or Dad breaks promises and denies the problems in the family that are difficult and painful to expose, children learn not to trust. Dad promises his children that on Sunday afternoon the whole family is going on a picnic in the country. Everyone becomes very excited and starts making plans about what they will wear, what food they will eat and which games they will play. When Sunday comes, Dad is in bed with a hangover from the night before, and he has decided to cancel the picnic. In fact, Dad cancels many family activities because of his alcoholism. Mom covers up for Dad by saying he has the flu, but the children know why Dad is sick because they have seen it before. These children by now have probably developed a survival tool that allows them to outlive the pain of broken promises and untrue excuses. This tool says, "If I don't trust, I don't have to get close. If

I don't get close, I don't have to risk feeling disappointment, pain, rejection, abandonment and shame."

In a dysfunctional family system, family members also learn to discount their own perception about what is taking place. When Mom says that Dad is sick with the flu, she not only is rejecting what she knows is the real problem, she also is renouncing what her children are seeing and feeling. This process of discounting the children's reality makes it difficult for them to trust others and themselves.

By nature children are self-centered. They see the world rotating around them, even as they enter adolescence. This perception is a normal part of the developmental process. Children also view Mom and Dad as the Higher Power because they are bigger and provide food, clothing, shelter, nurturance, love and emotional support. If Mom is a prescription drug addict and not emotionally available for her children, the children may develop a concept of a Higher Power that cannot always be trusted to be available. Children use magical thinking: if Mom is unavailable, the children may begin to believe that she isn't available because they are bad. The children's feeling of shame begins to build within to become a shame core. The children may act out with eating disorders, using chemicals, fighting at school, sleeping difficulties or regressing to earlier behavior such as bed-wetting.

Because of the three dysfunctional family rules: 1) **Don't talk about what is really going on,** 2) **Certain feelings are not acceptable,** and 3) **Don't trust — the world is not a safe place,** we find that bulimia is a way to turn off and shut down the pain around us. Many of us believed for years that one day everything would be **fixed** if we just ignored **it**. It is hopeful we eventually discover that we have a responsibility to ourselves to break these family rules. Breaking these long-standing rules does not have to do with not loving our families or blaming them, but instead with learning how the family system has impacted our lives in the past and continues to do so in the present. It is difficult, if not impossible, to change those ideas, values and behaviors that we are unaware of but nevertheless have. Many of us are not capable of making changes within our lives until we know what we need to alter. Beginning to explore the patterns in our family system is an appropriate place to start.

5

Recovering From Shame

My disease of bulimia covered up the shame I had felt as a young
adolescent. I continued to carry this shame, without choice, into adulthood.
It was compounded by my disease of chemical dependency. Then there
came a point in my life where for a split second I was able to look past the
shame and learn that I had choices. A very small spark of brightness within
my shame-based soul, which had allowed me to survive addiction, gave me
the courage to realize I was worthy of recovery. Today this same spark of life,
now much bigger and brighter, continues to guide me through my journey
in recovery.

It is important that we find that very small spark within because it is alive
and waiting to be recognized in all of us. This spark of life lets us know we
are worthy of recovery. Our small shining star can provide us with the
willingness to begin addressing those issues and feelings the disease of
bulimia covers up. Another guiding light that moves us toward recovery
from this disease is an open mind. An open mind can provide us with the
courage to learn, risk new behavior and grow. With an open mind and a
touch of willingness, the wheels of recovery begin to move forward. As we

continue to move forward, we find we can love ourselves, and it becomes difficult to return to self-destructive behavior.

Ultimately we learn how to be responsible for our eating behavior and treat our bodies with love and care. As we heal physically, emotionally and spiritually, we discover our body is not the enemy and that food can be an enjoyable part of life. With continued recovery, the unhealthy shame we have carried for years will be replaced with self-love. Recovery is a life-long adventure where we continue to grow and explore ourselves along with our world. As we grow, the spark of life within us also grows.

It became crucial for me to learn all I could about my addictions and how they were affecting my physical, mental, emotional and spiritual self. I had no idea how self-destructive my disease was for me and how it was affecting those around me.

There are a number of 12-Step programs in existence today that address addictive diseases and give support and information to individuals who are willing to make changes in their lives. There are: Alcoholics Anonymous (AA), Al-Anon, Co-dependents Anonymous, Overeaters Anonymous, Adult Children of Alcoholics, Emotions Anonymous, Sexual Addictions Anonymous, etc. These programs are based on 12 Steps that encourage individuals to ask for help and provide a set of healthy principles by which to live. These principles teach that it is possible to live successfully without addiction. The programs encourage continued growth and have been extremely successful in dealing with addictive disorders. As we begin learning about our addictions, participation in these programs will augment our newly found knowledge.

Within the last five years there has been a great deal of advancement in the area of treatment for eating disorders. Many professionals are beginning to view bulimia and other eating disorders as addictive diseases and are treating them as such.

Loving ourselves enough to commit to treatment is truly a way we can begin our recovery. Treatment is strongly recommended because most bulimics can benefit from it.

Guidelines For Finding Inpatient Treatment

Some guidelines for looking into inpatient treatment for eating disorders are:

1. **Is the program based on the 12 Steps of Overeaters Anonymous, Co-dependents Anonymous, etc.?**

2. **Does the staff believe and follow the disease concept in relationship to eating disorders and treat bulimia as an addiction?**

3. **Is the staff in recovery and participating in recovery programs?**

I remember working as a professional with addictive disorders before having addressed my own issues. It was difficult for me to see with clarity what was going on with the patients with whom I was working. My personal belief is that professionals in the field of addiction need to be working on their own recovery on a continuous basis in order to keep a clean mental house. Otherwise, it is difficult for the professionals to have objectivity. It also can be impossible for them to understand the difficulties their clients are experiencing because of their own denial.

4. **Does the program have an extensive aftercare program?**

Treatment can provide the tools for recovery, but the real work usually takes place after treatment. Aftercare is necessary in that it bridges the gap between the safe world of treatment and the unpredictable realities of real life.

5. **What is the program's policy on medication — is medication encouraged or discouraged?**

As mentioned earlier, it was important for me to realize that my feelings were a part of me that I needed to begin experiencing them for my own growth. In some programs medication is given when not necessary. Many individuals with eating disorders have become cross-addicted to mood-altering chemicals as a result of going to professionals who are uneducated about addictions and prescribed tranquilizers, antidepressants, sleeping pills, stimulants, etc. This compounds and confuses the problem, creating more barriers to recovery. Mood-altering medication can prevent one from experiencing those feelings and related issues that are the essence of recovery.

A very few individuals may need medication; thus, it is important to know whether or not the medical doctor for the program has an understanding of the addiction process. A few doctors have a specialty in addictive disorders. Those programs that limit the use of mood-altering medication usually do so because they follow the disease concept. Major concerns include shopping around and asking questions when looking for inpatient treatment. You are the consumer; it is *your* life. You merit the best in available treatment.

6. **Is there a family component to the program?**

Family members of bulimics needs treatment just as desperately as the identified patient. I did not marry a co-dependent mate by accident. Those of us who have grown up in dysfunctional families tend to seek out, on an unconscious basis, individuals similar to our own family of origin. Those of us still living in our family of origin are a part of an entire dysfunctional system that needs help. The program should encourage the participation of as many family members as possible. A healthy recovery center usually includes a week long family program as part of the treatment process and encourages family members to attend 12-Step support groups for their own recovery.

7. **How long does the inpatient program last?**

Healthy programs usually are an average of 42 days in length. Programs that continue over many months are probably not geared toward responsible recovery. Treatment provides the tools for recovery. If extended care is necessary, there are a number of halfway programs that can bridge the gap between treatment and returning to families, jobs and school. Programs that do not refer to halfway programs or that encourage long-term stay should be questioned.

Outpatient Treatment

Outpatient therapy also can be beneficial for the bulimic who has started to realize bulimia is a problem. Until I had begun to break through some of the denial regarding my bulimia and had developed a touch of motivation, therapy on an outpatient basis was a waste of the therapist's time and my money. It is impossible to work with alcoholics or drug addicts who are not willing to address their chemical usage. This also holds true for the bulimic who is not willing to address the eating disorder. *Willingness* is a pre-requisite for outpatient therapy.

Therapist

It also is important to select a therapist who is involved in his or her own recovery process. A large number of professionals in the helping fields come from dysfunctional families where their own family-of-origin role was that of a helper; as a result, they may be untreated co-dependents or addicted persons. If the therapist discourages certain feelings, doesn't address the addiction or family-of-origin issues and is not very supportive of 12-Step programs, most likely he or she is limited in terms of skills and information necessary for dealing with bulimia. Many untreated professionals set themselves up as the only solution and avoid recovery workshops, lectures and support. This can become an issue for the client who may become dependent on the therapist without other involvement. The client may then set the therapist up as a Higher Power. As a result of this, growth can be difficult to achieve. Shopping around for an appropriate therapist should be a priority. If the relationship does not feel right, talk to others. If necessary, move on. You are the consumer, and this is about your recovery. Otherwise, outpatient therapy can be an invaluable growth experience with the therapist as a teacher and guide.

Group Therapy

Group therapy can be very powerful as well as the least expensive of the therapy processes. In group situations, not only does one receive feedback from the therapist but also from other group participants. The group process can be a very exciting, challenging and nurturing experience. This process allows one the opportunity to develop communication skills and begin addressing those issues that have not been resolved as a result of addiction. Group therapy makes it possible for us to break the no talk rule that kept so many of us from feeling our feelings and learning how to trust.

A healthy group consists of members who work 12-Step programs and a facilitator who does the same. For some, individual therapy for a period of time before a group experience can be a bridge, allowing trust issues to be addressed. Group experiences are a major factor in healthy recovery.

6

Where To Begin

Food journals can be invaluable for beginning recovery. The type of food journal referred to here is not concerned with calculating calories. Many of us can calculate the total number of calories we have consumed in one day in about 30 seconds. Instead this journal focuses on feelings and our avoidance of them. As a bulimic, I have spent a great deal of time avoiding the pain in my life by obsessing on food, calories and my weight. The food journal began to direct my attention to what I was avoiding as a result of my eating disorder.

Sample Food Journals

Before eating breakfast. I woke up at seven o'clock from a bad dream and felt depressed but couldn't remember all of the dream.

Eating breakfast. I ate cereal, eggs (2), toast (2), juice, coffee. I felt numb while I ate.

After eating breakfast. I had a lot of anxiety. I felt fat. I threw up. Shame and depression followed. I binged on cereal and threw up again. Then I felt numb.

What do you think was being avoided? In the example on p. 29, something about the dream was causing this individual a great deal of anxiety and depression. As a result of binging and purging it is difficult to extract and process information involving the dream that could have been of great value.

Before eating lunch. I was so angry with my boss but couldn't tell him so. I felt really abused and unimportant.

Eating lunch. I went to lunch but ended up binging on chips and dip. I didn't eat my usual lunch and felt a lot of shame. I stopped by the drug store and bought two candy bars and ate them on the way back to the office. Then I felt depressed and wanted to isolate.

After eating. I made a decision to jog an extra five miles after work today.

In this example it is pretty obvious that the individual has a difficult time with anger, especially in relationship to authority. As a result of not being able to confront the boss, the process of self-destruction begins by not eating a healthy lunch. This form of self-punishment is continued with eating the candy bars and exercising excessively. The anger is stuffed with food and exercise, and the chance for growth cannot be utilized.

Before eating. I received a phone call from my soon-to-be ex-husband. It has been a hard couple of months. Also I weighed myself this morning and realized I had gained five pounds. I felt incredibly fat and ugly.

Eating. I continued my strict diet of grapefruit, hard boiled eggs and dill pickles. I hate dill pickles. An hour later I went to the store and bought a bag of cookies and some popcorn. I ate half the bag of cookies and the bag of popcorn. I felt like a failure, worthless and depressed.

After eating. I have made a decision to try three times as hard to stick to my diet of grapefruit, hard boiled eggs and dill pickles.

This woman will not be able to work through the grief process involving her upcoming divorce. Her attention is too focused on her eating disorder, and it appears easier to focus on the dieting more than on the pain of separation. As a result of this, she may never resolve the relationship.

Benefits Of The Food Journal

The food journal allows us to begin to see what feelings and issues we are avoiding as a result of bulimia. I found by keeping a journal that every time

I was angry, I would end up in front of the refrigerator looking for something to eat. I did not know how to be angry and had learned to stuff it with food. My journal enabled me to get in touch with my anger, and eventually I developed the tools for processing it.

The journal also indicated that there were certain times of the day that were more stressful. During these times I discovered I was more prone to binging. For some, nighttime can be the most difficult; for others, it may be in the morning or only on weekends. I also discovered that when I was around certain individuals I was more prone to binging. Once we have an idea of what times or in what situations we are most vulnerable, we can begin to process those issues related to our behavior and make some positive changes. For some, the change may be attending 12-Step meetings during these times or calling a group member or sponsor.

The food journal also permits us to take a look at our eating patterns. Until I knew what my pattern was, I couldn't change it. At times I would eat standing up or in my car and, on some occasions, even in bed. I discovered that I had difficulty eating at the dinner table. This bit of information enabled me to tap many unresolved issues I had never addressed that were causing me pain. I started eating at the table and let myself feel my feelings. Today I can enjoy a meal at the table while feeling quite comfortable. This is a result of allowing myself to experience fear, anger, sadness, loneliness and shame without covering up.

7

Where To Go And What To Look For

For my recovery it also was helpful for me to have a picture of what my entire family looked like as a system so that I could learn a bit more about myself and my addictions. Every piece of information I have discovered has been a gift and beneficial to my recovery.

While growing up in my family, I had learned about being female by observing the women, and I had learned about males by observing the men. I had learned about relationships by observing the members of my family interact and had developed many behaviors, values and opinions as a result of these experiences. By taking a good hard look at where I came from and how I grew up, I was able to begin healing old wounds and understanding my family. I also was able to decide which behaviors, values and opinions from my family of origin I agreed with and to change those that did not fit for me. This process was my taking responsibility for myself and my recovery.

Family-Of-Origin Issues

It is important for the reader to realize that examining family-of-origin issues (those unresolved issues involving our parents, siblings, grandparents, aunts and uncles) is not about searching for whom or what to blame. Looking at these issues allows us to see how our families have impacted on our lives and helps us to understand our families and who we are. By exploring our family-of-origin issues, we are accepting responsibility for our recovery and the changes that are necessary for our growth. Entire families heal as a result of this; therefore, exploration in this area is strongly encouraged. In many cases when one member begins the journey, it inspires others to begin the process of recovery.

In my family of origin I had learned that it was possible for me to avoid my feelings of pain, isolation, fear and shame by participating in the disease of bulimia. When I began reaching for recovery, I discovered that it was necessary for me to turn back the hands of time to see what unresolved pain I was still carrying from my past. Before I could let go and move on, I needed to find out what unfinished business from childhood was still within me. Once I had addressed those issues, I was open for the experiences, lessons and gifts of the present.

Family Secrets

In dysfunctional family systems there are usually a number of secrets and topics that are rarely discussed. When these secrets are not acknowledged and resolved by those involved, family members will act them out. If Mom is bulimic and Dad knows something is wrong but won't get help or talk about it, Dad may begin avoiding his feelings by putting in more overtime at work, thereby evading Mom's disease. The kids, sensing something is wrong with Mom and Dad, may begin feeling and believing that their parents are experiencing difficulties as a result of them or something they have done. In reality, Dad is having a difficult time with his feelings about Mom's bulimia, and Mom is preoccupied with her addiction. Neither of them can talk about their feelings because their awareness about addiction and its treatment is limited. They cannot see clearly what is happening, both being in denial of the seriousness of the dysfunction in the family.

In an alcoholic family, members will blame excessive alcohol usage for problems at work, family pressure, etc., instead of facing the feelings involved with admitting a loved one is suffering from the disease of alcoholism. This process of avoidance and denial is similar for the disease of bulimia or any family secret.

In the example of the family affected by the disease of bulimia, Dad continues to distance himself from the home as a way to avoid looking at how the disease of bulimia is influencing the family. As a result the kids may begin to feel rejected, abandoned and angry. Because Mom also is committed in keeping her disease a secret and because it is not being discussed or resolved, the kids may begin acting out their feelings at school through failing grades, drug or alcohol abuse, fighting or other self-destructive behaviors. If we ignore our feelings or do not feel safe enough to talk about them, they will eventually surface in the form of dysfunctional behavior.

For successful recovery, it is crucial to look at family secrets in order to determine how they have impacted our lives. We need to begin exploring whether or not these unresolved issues from the past are influencing our thoughts and behaviors in present day life. In some cases, we may find ourselves repeating the secrets that previous generations refused to discuss and resolve. If secrets are not exposed and resolved, they often are repeated by other family members. I have seen families repeat secrets from one generation to the next, not being aware until recovery that the secrets were even there because they were never discussed.

It also is important to look at who was involved in the secret and to explore why it wasn't acceptable to talk about it. Many do not feel safe asking family members about family-of-origin issues; therefore, we should begin this process with what we know. Then this will lead us to what we don't know. We usually have more information than we realize. It can involve memories and experiences we have either previously dismissed or ignored. Once we begin thinking about how our family history is currently affecting us, we can discover a wealth of information. This process of discovery is like putting together a big jigsaw puzzle and finally seeing how all of the little pieces fit.

How To Address Family Secrets

To address family secrets we might begin looking for the following missing pieces:

1. Eating disorders — what kind, overweight, underweight (who and where)
2. Alcohol problems (who and when)
3. Drug difficulties — legal or illegal (who, when, what)
4. Physical abuse (who, when, how)
5. Sexual abuse (who, when, how)
6. Sexual acting out — extramarital affairs (who and when)
7. Gambling problems (who, when and how)
8. Employment difficulties (who and when)
9. Legal problems (who, when, what)
10. Physical illnesses (who, when, what)

We might also want to ask these questions:

1. What did anger look like in my family? How was anger handled?
2. Was it safe to cry in my family?
3. Was sex ever discussed and how?
4. How was death handled in my family? Was it discussed? Did my family allow grieving?
5. What was discussed at the dinner table? Was it safe to talk about anything? Was dinner time comfortable or uncomfortable?
6. What other topics were not discussed in my family? Why?

It is suggested that this process of exploration be done with the support of those in 12-Step groups and a therapist who understands the impact of family-of-origin issues.

Compiling A Family Tree

It may also be valuable to have a visual picture of what the entire family system looks like. This can be accomplished by putting together a family tree. (See Figures 7.1 and 7.2).

As a result of constructing a family tree, we are able to take a look at what we already know about our family of origin. Before looking at what I did know, I spent a great deal of time trying to solve the issues for which I had very little information. By completing a family tree, I was able to see many patterns of behavior in my family that had been active for a couple of generations. How I viewed myself as a woman was the result of repeating patterns of behavior I had inherited from my mother. In turn she had inherited these same behavior patterns and concepts regarding her role as a female from her mother, my grandmother.

In preparing a family tree, aside from seeing the patterns of behavior and possible addiction, we also can ask ourselves what each member was like and how each has influenced our lives. Did we like them or not? Were they easy to talk to or distant? Were they warm and accepting or critical and difficult to please? Could we trust them and feel safe sharing our feelings or did we know they were not to be trusted? We can begin our exploration by finding four to five adjectives that really describe each family member. We also might compare them to one another to see what common ideas and values made them a family with an identity. It also is significant to look at those characteristics that defined them individually within the system.

Figure 7.1 A Sample Family Tree

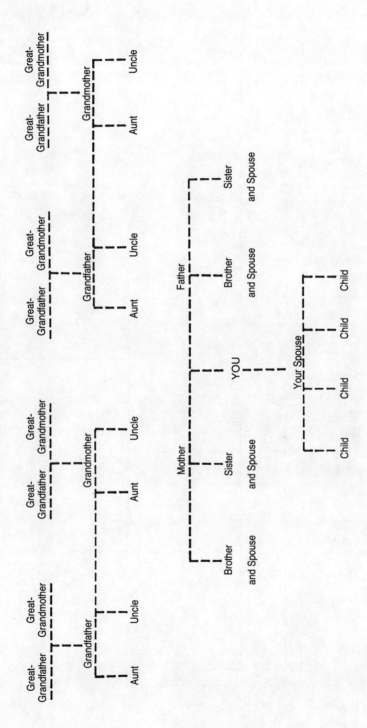

Figure 7.2 Your Family Tree

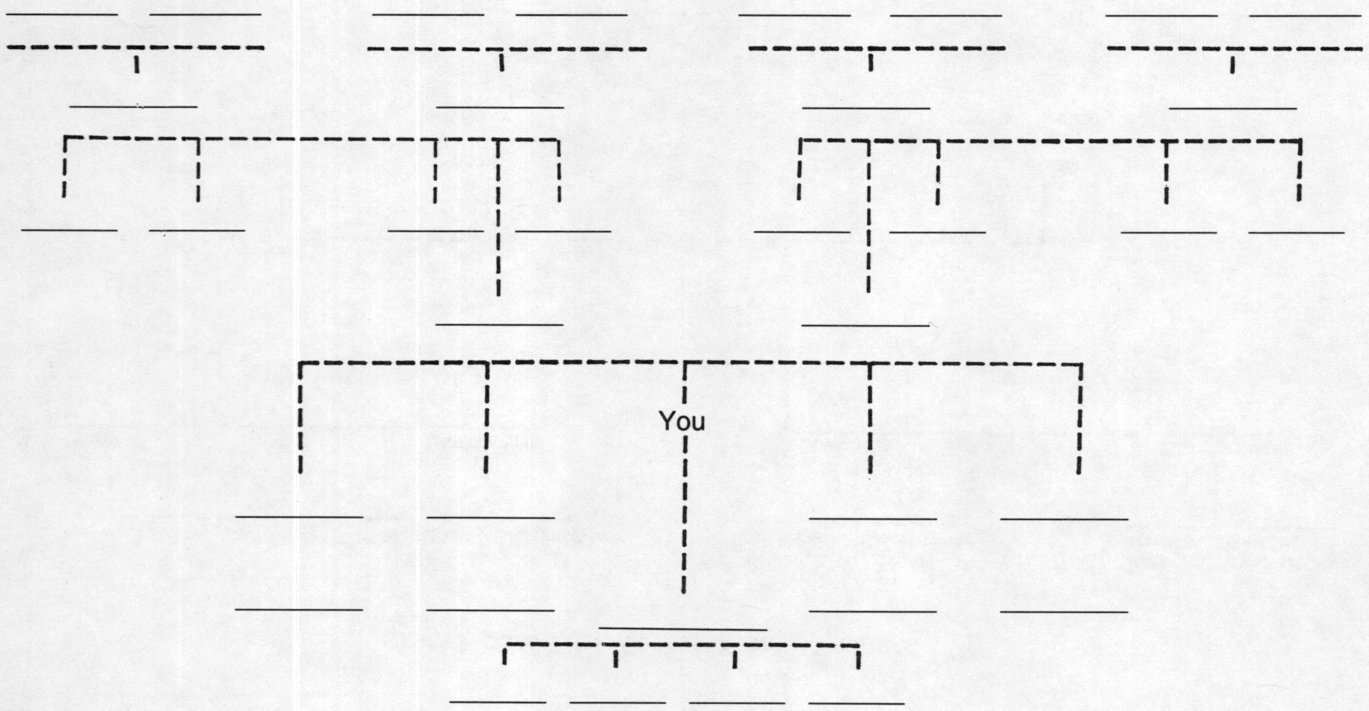

Patterns Of Family Behavior

These are a few of the questions we might address as we put our family tree together:

1. If boys and girls were treated differently, how was this done?
2. What were some of the family traditions around holidays, birthdays and other gatherings?
3. How did heritage affect the family?
4. How were family disagreements handled?
5. Was there one member who seemed to be in charge of the whole family?
6. Who had more power in the family, the men or the women?
7. Who were the disciplinarians of the children and of the family in general?
8. Were there expectations of behavior in the family?
9. How were children disciplined?
10. What did it mean to be male in the family?
11. What did it mean to be female?

Family Physical Characteristics

Also, we should note any physical characteristics that were specific for members such as physical defects, birthmarks, excess height, shortness, weight (over or under), etc. Many physical characteristics can influence one's self-esteem and perception of self. For example, I am six-feet tall; as a young five-foot-ten adolescent, I felt different from the other girls at school. As a result of being so tall, I felt that I was not as pretty as the shorter girls and felt less acceptable. I believe that my inability to accept my height contributed to my eating disorder and the shame I felt about my body.

Overcoming Memory Loss

If the relationship feels safe with brothers or sisters, it is helpful to talk with them about the family of origin. Their perceptions of growing up may provide valuable information that can aid in piecing together the family puzzle. Occasionally brothers and sisters can fill in those blank areas of our memory. They may say something that triggers a memory to fill the gap or even produce a memory that was previously unknown. They can add to our awareness and provide some of the unknowns.

For some of us, there may be memory loss as a result of growing up in a painful environment where there was some form of trauma. In instances of emotional, physical or sexual abuse, children may disassociate or "shut down" in a number of ways as a means of surviving a threatening situation. This shutting down is the mind's way of protecting itself and making survival in the family system possible. Memory can be recalled slowly as a result of sharing with those safe members in our family of origin. If you have experienced emotional, physical or sexual abuse and begin recalling such instances, it is strongly recommended that you find the support of a therapist who can guide you through a process of healing.

Clarification Of Family History With Photographs

To continue recovering from our addiction, we need to commit ourselves to further growth, even if it is painful. Part of this growth process involves getting our history straight. We should understand where we came from and how our family has influenced us.

A tool that can aid in putting the pieces of our life together are photographs of family members and ourselves. For example, I sat down one day with a number of photographs of myself, put them in chronological order and found that they aided my memory and also allowed me to understand at what point my bulimia began. As I continued this process, I was able to recall events and experiences from the past that previously I had not thought about or acknowledged. Each picture from my childhood had a story to tell, permitting me to reconnect visually with my past. Having another person, such as a therapist, group member or friend in recovery, look at the photographs can offer new insights. A second opinion may validate what we see or may offer other possibilities that we may not have considered.

Using photographs as a topic of discussion may feel safer when collecting family-of-origin information from family members. Photos may provide more information than expected about the events associated with the time the picture was taken. Be aware of the feelings that surface while examining photographs. Note which pictures evoke sadness, depression, fear or loneliness and which produce feelings of warmth, joy, safety and love. Feelings usually tell the truth; therefore, we should trust what surfaces when exploring family albums.

By studying our family photographs, we may be able to see patterns of behavior among family members. In addition we can begin to discover how we fit into the system and what our roles were. The experience of reliving some of our past can provide us with information about the issues we still need to address as well as the changes we need to make for our recovery. The experiences of the past can provide the tools for the present. Exploring our family of origin can result in many gifts for us and our recovery.

8

Recovery: A Gift Of Life

Recovery is a gift of life because prior to recovery many of us are just surviving. I always felt like an outside observer to life and wondered if I would ever feel a part of the world around me. While in my addictions, I felt disconnected and did not believe that it was possible for me to know what it felt like to be truly alive. My addictions separated me from knowing myself and the world around me. Today I participate in the life experience with a feeling of being capable of connecting with self, humanity and nature.

I also am able to function in life with the aid of healthy tools that not only enable me to appreciate the feelings of joy and peace of mind, but also allow me to move through painful times that are a natural product of the life process. New problems provide challenge and a chance for growth while new experiences provide opportunity and the lessons of life. Today I no longer need to run to an addiction because I am learning how to live and function in the school of life.

Time, Commitment And Willingness

Recovery from the disease of bulimia or any addiction takes time, commitment and willingness. We spend a great deal of time in addiction

41

and behavior that is destructive to our physical, emotional and spiritual well-being. When we reach for recovery, the majority of us do not know how to avoid being self-destructive. Adapting to healthy behavior can seem foreign and difficult because it initially feels unnatural. The strong shame core bulimics carry can entice us into believing we are not worth the time, effort, patience and love that recovery demands. However, if we are gentle with ourselves and trust the recovery process, we can learn to care for ourselves with the realization we are worthwhile and valuable.

Healing Physically

An important aspect of beginning recovery is healing physically. The human body is a complex biological organism in which the disease of bulimia can cause disruption and imbalance. Our moods can be influenced by the chemistry of our bodies, and it is crucial that we begin to care for our delicate physical self. Some of us need the aid of treatment or medical personnel to regain a physical balance because we have depleted ourselves of essential vitamins, minerals and nutrients as a result of bulimia. Many of us have little understanding of healthy eating behavior and may have to take time to learn how to eat all over again.

I never did discover what it meant to eat like a lady, but I believe that today my eating patterns are healthier than those developed during childhood. I have found that by eating responsibly my body is able to do what it was naturally designed to do with less stress and less susceptibility to illness. I can eat a variety of foods and feel satisfied after completing a balanced meal without feeling cheated and a desire to binge. I do not follow any strict diet because I believe that diets can be an antecedent for binging behavior. I do avoid a few foods I abused while in bulimia and hope that someday I will feel comfortable eating them in a healthy manner. I have not gained hundreds of pounds as a result of recovery and am at a comfortable body weight for my height and bone structure. I do not have a scale in my home because I believe it can become a part of the obsessive behavior found in bulimia. I have seen a scale control the mood of some bulimics for days and feel that weighing one's self daily can perpetuate the addiction. If necessary, I will weigh myself at a doctor's office.

If we feel a need to lose a couple of pounds, it is important that we get a reality check with our therapist, group members or recovery friends because most bulimics have an inappropriate concept of their body size. Our recovery friends will usually give us honest feedback. If we begin to see ourselves feeling shame after we eat or if we begin binging and return to old bulimic patterns, it is urgent that we see these behaviors as signals to us that there are unresolved issues we need to address. At these times we must keep a food journal and contact support systems.

Today when I exercise it can be a choice and not a compulsion. As a result of recovery, I have experimented with yoga, snorkling and rowing and would like to try wind surfing, scuba diving and ice skating. I have discovered that exercise can be enjoyable when it is not compulsive and that it can take on many forms. If I miss several days or even a week of exercising, it is not the end of the world because I know that in time I will return to my program or activity of exercise. If we begin to feel compulsive about exercising, it's important to begin looking at what feelings are coming up and why we want to cover them up.

Focusing On Emotional Self

Once on the road toward physical health and recovery, we can begin to focus on our emotional self. As we continue our recovery process from the disease of bulimia, those feelings we have avoided with addiction will begin to surface. Also, we will start remembering bits and pieces of our past. While recalling past memories and experiencing the feelings associated with them, we will gain a better understanding of our family-of-origin issues. Developing a clearer picture of what these issues are, we can decide which ones still need resolution. Once the problems are identified, we can work on their resolution. This may be a confusing time as we discover what our feelings are and how they are related to present and past issues. Being part of a recovering group for validation and support is necessary during those times when we are unclear about our feelings.

Experiencing Growth

Moving through our past unfinished business and family-of-origin issues, we will begin to discover pieces of ourselves that we like. We will see that we are worth loving and getting to know. Furthermore, we will learn that we have choices and that those behaviors or qualities we dislike about ourselves can be changed. The child inside each of us needs to be nurtured and cared for, and we can learn how to be our own best friend and parent. Taking responsibility for our recovery and who we are, we will start to care for ourselves in ways that are healthy and loving.

On completion of our unfinished business and unresolved family-of-origin issues, we will find that we have more time and room within for those life experiences we have always wanted. We will be able to experience life in the present and live each moment to its fullest potential. I always thought life would be better tomorrow, but when tomorrow came I would be too preoccupied with next week to live in the moment. While cleaning away our unfinished business, we will discover that we are problem solving and developing a number of healthy tools to replace our ineffective past behaviors and survival techniques. Our relationships with family and friends may improve, reaching new, healthy levels of understanding as we realize progress and growth. We no longer need to be hampered or hindered from knowing who we are.

Most of us have been living in a very limited world while in our addiction. In recovery we see the horizons broaden with each growth period. Through growth, we comprehend that there are no patent answers and that experience is the best teacher. To return to bulimia or any addiction after experiencing recovery means cutting ourselves off from growth. As we learn how to live life in recovery, we will have a hard time imagining how we found time to obsess on our addiction because today life is full from sunrise to sunset. With experience and risk taking with others comes trust. We share ourselves on a deeper level with friends and family, letting them know who we really are. We never have to be alone with our pain again, unless we choose to be. We can let others know what we are feeling as a result of learning it is no longer necessary to hide behind a false sense of well-being.

Developing Spiritually

Spiritually we begin to develop as we connect with life and those around us. We may discover our creative self and explore or rediscover crafts, the arts, gardening, hobbies and other activities that bulimia had pushed aside. We also can connect with our own individual concept of a Higher Power and nurturing our spiritual self. It is difficult to have a healthy spiritual relationship with a Higher Power until we deal with our unfinished business. Once we resolve old issues, learn to love ourselves and realize others value who we are, we will start to realize that there is a loving Higher Power.

The first part of our being that is affected by addiction is the loss of our spiritual self. Next emotional health is endangered. Finally we suffer the physical consequences of dependency. What a high price to pay!

We can never truly know who we really are or what our potential is while we are involved in addiction. Addictions separate us from ourselves, others and a Higher Power. Life cannot be seen clearly or experienced fully as long as it is filtered through alcoholism, drug addiction, bulimia, anorexia, sexual addiction, workaholism or any other obsessive compulsive disorder. With recovery, we can see clearly, feel freely and experience the most from each moment we are here on this earth. Life is for the living, but we cannot be fully aware and alive if we are numbed by addiction. When you decide to accept and appreciate your self-worth, you will be able to experience life.

PART

2

Exercises For Overcoming Bulimia

Introduction

When I finally made a commitment to my own personal recovery from the disease of bulimia, one of the first things I was told to do was to write. When I asked what I was supposed to write about, I was told to write about my feelings. At this point, I remember being very confused because I didn't know what my feelings were. Therefore, I didn't understand how I could write about them. It also was suggested that I begin writing about my past life difficulties and resentments. But I had a lot of memory loss and my past was very confusing to me. I would become frustrated and angry while focusing on not being able to remember and end up not writing at all. Then I directed my attention toward those difficulties in my present life and decided that this was what I would write about.

My view of life, which was an attitude of either all or nothing and black or white, kept me from seeing life as it really was. I would become angry, depressed and confused because my recovery seemed so overwhelming, and my life as I viewed it appeared to make little, if any, sense.

After sitting at the kitchen table and feeling intimidated with pencil in hand as I stared at a blank piece of paper for an hour or so, I would give up. I would then feel shame for not knowing how to write. Eventually, after repeating this pattern several times, I decided there must be an easier way.

What I discovered was that I needed some guidelines for writing and that there were many available. I searched through workbooks and recovery readings, picking those writing techniques that worked for me. These techniques and guidelines gave me direction as to what to write about. They also directed me toward writing about what I did know instead of focusing on what I didn't know or couldn't remember. Writing became less intimidating and eventually evolved into a wonderful tool that I continue to use in my recovery program on a consistent basis.

It is hopeful that these exercises will provide you with guidelines and directions in writing. I believe that taking the time to write about our present life situations and past family-of-origin issues is essential for personal exploration and growth in recovery from addiction. Here are a number of topics that address those issues we may find difficult to write about or may not have considered. These are ideas intended to encourage further exploration. This section will not provide the answers because I believe our answers come from within, but it will be a step toward the answers. If we are willing to question who we are and become committed to finding the answer, the following pages can be the start of an exciting life-long journey.

My support is with you as you begin your own journey toward self-discovery. I encourage you to find strength and wisdom as you continue along the road of recovery from bulimia.

9

The Food Journal: A Way In

Before I began my recovery from bulimia, there were days when I couldn't remember what I had eaten or even when I had eaten. On many occasions I would find myself eating without having given it any thought. I remember being at a large social gathering, listening to a very heated political discussion between several people that involved a great deal of disagreement. I do not remember having any feelings about the topic of discussion. Then, at one point during the conversation, I looked down at a vegetable platter that had been sitting next to me and realized I had eaten half of it in a very short period of time. It was as if I had been in a fog while eating and as a result of this fog had experienced an emotional blackout.

On a different occasion I was at a small dinner party and noticed that one of the other guests appeared to be angry with the host. The two seemed to be engaged in a disagreement of some sort at the end of the dining table. Before I knew it, I had finished my salad before the other guests had even begun. I remember feeling embarrassed and shameful as I reached for another dinner roll, hoping no one had noticed my rapid eating behavior. As a result of being so focused on my behavior with food I was not able to address the issues of my inability to deal with anger or disagreement. I had used food to avoid my feelings about the disagreement taking place at the other end of the table and had been totally unaware of it.

For my recovery, it was necessary to begin taking a look at what I ate and how I ate. Did I eat during stressful times? What feelings did I cover up with my eating? How did my obsession with food interfere with my ability to deal with reality? In what ways did my eating disorder keep me from knowing myself? How was my disease cheating me out of the growth process and life in general?

Recording Eating Patterns

A food journal can be invaluable in helping us to begin looking at our eating patterns. Once we have made a commitment to exploring our eating patterns, we can then take a look at how our behavior keeps us from experiencing our feelings. With a food journal we can begin focusing on those feelings and situations that cause us to behave in unhealthy ways instead of on the food we eat.

A food journal involves itemizing what foods we eat during the day. We also list with each meal and with any between-meal eating how we felt *before, during* and *after* eating. We can include in our journal those situations that caused us stress and made us eat. Taking a look at how we use food in unhealthy ways can release those feelings we avoid. In other words, with a food journal we can begin addressing what is really going on underneath the food usage instead of being preoccupied with counting calories or worrying about how long it will take to exercise off our unwanted pounds. A food journal does take a commitment of time, but the reward is a better understanding of self. This is a worthwhile process; it is suggested that a commitment of seven days be made for the first food journal.

Seven Feelings To Focus On In The Food Journal

For our purposes we will be focusing on seven specific feelings when writing in our journal. These seven feelings are *anger, pain, shame, joy, sadness, fear* and *numbness.* I have included numbness because I believe it is a feeling that often disguises other feelings. It is important that we begin addressing the significance of feeling numb instead of discounting it. I remember being extremely frustrated with myself when feeling numb. I would tell myself that I must be doing something wrong in my feeling work and that numbness was the result. In reality I was feeling numb for a reason. Sometimes we feel numb because it is not safe to experience the underlying feelings. By giving ourselves permission to feel numb, we are acknowledging our need for safety or we are taking care of ourselves. As we begin to feel more secure with ourselves and our recovery, the numbness tends to disappear, allowing the underlying feelings to surface. Remember that we all move at our own individual pace and that feelings are neither right nor wrong. They just are. We can get from the food journal only what we are willing to put into it. Table 9.1 and Table 9.2 demonstrate what a food journal might look like after a couple days of committed writing. Can you see what feelings are being avoided?

Tables 9.3-9.9 are for you to use as you log seven days of food intake and feelings related to eating. Complete them as you continue on the road to recovery.

Determining Eating Patterns

After spending seven days on our food journal, it is important for us to go back through the week and begin looking for eating patterns. One pattern I discovered was that I would eat when confronted with angry people or situations. I also found that my eating disorder kept me from experiencing my own anger. Every time I began experiencing anger, I would find myself standing in front of the refrigerator looking for something to eat.

Many of us discover that we tend to become involved in our eating disorder during certain times of the day. Or, we might find that we binge while in certain situations. We may begin seeing that during stressful times we become more obsessed with our exercise programs and bodies. We may discover that we behave appropriately with food during breakfast and lunch only to totally lose all control at dinnertime. We may notice that we can eat normally for several days and binge periodically on other days. Some of us may binge in isolation, when alone and withdrawn from our friends and loved ones. Others of us may begin seeing that our binging behavior is a consistent activity.

I found that I could binge on anything, whereas others would only binge on specific foods. Many of us may discover that there are certain foods that trigger our binging behavior the way the first drink for an alcoholic can set off a drinking spree.

It is important that we begin listing our eating patterns and obsessive actions around food, our thinking about food, our exercising and other related behaviors. Once we identify these behaviors we can begin to consciously choose whether or not we wish to continue them. At this time we also can make decisions about how we would like to change our eating patterns and obsessive behavior with food, calories, pounds, exercising, scales and our bodies.

Table 9.1. Sample Food Journal

	Feelings* before Eating	List and Quantity of Foods Eaten	Feelings* while Eating	Feelings* after Eating	Situations of Significance before or while Eating
Breakfast	Joy	Two eggs on toast Orange juice	Joy	Joy	Heard the day before I was getting a raise
Other**	Fear	Coffee Sweet roll	Numbness	Numbness	Heard a rumor I wasn't getting a raise
Lunch	Anger	Hamburger and Salad Milk shake Potato chips	Numbness Sadness	Anger	Heard from boss I wasn't getting a raise
Other**	Sadness	One half bag of cookies	Numbness	Numbness	Decided I would work out at gym for an extra two hours
Dinner	Skipped Dinner				
Other**	Sadness Anger	Two pieces of cake Dip Popcorn	Numbness Sadness Shame	Shame	Did 100 situps before bed

* *Feelings* to focus on are **anger, pain, shame, joy, sadness, fear** and **numbness.**
**Other refers to food eaten between meals.

Table 9.2. Another Sample Food Journal

	Feelings* before Eating	List and Quantity of Foods Eaten	Feelings* while Eating	Feelings* after Eating	Situations of Significance before or while Eating
Breakfast	Sadness Pain	Coffee Oatmeal Toast	Numbness	Sadness Threw up breakfast	Sad dream last night about my childhood
Other**	Pain Sadness	Two doughnuts	Numbness	Pain Shame Threw up	Felt shame about not knowing how to quit throwing up
Lunch	Numbness	Salad Corn chips Diet soda	Numbness Pain	Pain Sadness	Friend cancelled a dinner engagement
Other**	Numbness Sadness	Two candy bars	Numbness	Shame Numbness Threw up	Upset with self for eating two candy bars
Dinner	Sadness Pain	Piece of chicken Peas Potatoes	Sadness	Sadness	Ate dinner all alone
Other**	Numbness Sadness	Popcorn Ice cream Two apples	Numbness Sadness Shame	Angry Threw up	Angry at self for throwing up

* *Feelings* to focus on are **anger, pain, shame, joy, sadness, fear** and **numbness**.
**Other* refers to food eaten between meals.

Table 9.3. Food Journal: Day One

	Feelings* before Eating	List and Quantity of Foods Eaten	Feelings* while Eating	Feelings* after Eating	Situations of Significance before or while Eating
Breakfast					
Other**					
Lunch					
Other**					
Dinner					
Other**					

* *Feelings* to focus on are **anger, pain, shame, joy, sadness, fear and numbness.**
** *Other* refers to food eaten between meals.

Table 9.4. Food Journal: Day Two

	Feelings* before Eating	List and Quantity of Foods Eaten	Feelings* while Eating	Feelings* after Eating	Situations of Significance before or while Eating
Breakfast					
Other**					
Lunch					
Other**					
Dinner					
Other**					

* *Feelings* to focus on are **anger, pain, shame, joy, sadness, fear** and **numbness.**
**Other refers to food eaten between meals.

Table 9.5. Food Journal: Day Three

	Feelings* before Eating	List and Quantity of Foods Eaten	Feelings* while Eating	Feelings* after Eating	Situations of Significance before or while Eating
Breakfast					
Other**					
Lunch					
Other**					
Dinner					
Other**					

* Feelings to focus on are **anger, pain, shame, joy, sadness, fear** and **numbness.**
**Other refers to food eaten between meals.

Table 9.6. Food Journal: Day Four

	Feelings* before Eating	List and Quantity of Foods Eaten	Feelings* while Eating	Feelings* after Eating	Situations of Significance before or while Eating
Breakfast					
Other**					
Lunch					
Other**					
Dinner					
Other**					

* *Feelings* to focus on are **anger, pain, shame, joy, sadness, fear and numbness.**
** *Other* refers to food eaten between meals.

Table 9.7. Food Journal: Day Five

	Feelings* before Eating	List and Quantity of Foods Eaten	Feelings* while Eating	Feelings* after Eating	Situations of Significance before or while Eating
Breakfast					
*Other***					
Lunch					
*Other***					
Dinner					
*Other***					

* *Feelings* to focus on are **anger, pain, shame, joy, sadness, fear and numbness.**
** *Other* refers to food eaten between meals.

Table 9.8. Food Journal: Day Six

	Feelings* before Eating	List and Quantity of Foods Eaten	Feelings* while Eating	Feelings* after Eating	Situations of Significance before or while Eating
Breakfast					
Other**					
Lunch					
Other**					
Dinner					
Other**					

* *Feelings* to focus on are **anger, pain, shame, joy, sadness, fear and numbness.**
**Other* refers to food eaten between meals.

Table 9.9. Food Journal: Day Seven

	Feelings* before Eating	List and Quantity of Foods Eaten	Feelings* while Eating	Feelings* after Eating	Situations of Significance before or while Eating
Breakfast					
Other**					
Lunch					
Other**					
Dinner					
Other**					

* *Feelings* to focus on are **anger, pain, shame, joy, sadness, fear and numbness.**
** *Other* refers to food eaten between meals.

I discovered that I would eat to avoid my anger, only to end up feeling shame about having eaten in an inappropriate way. I would focus on my distress about eating and would lose contact with my anger. As a result of doing a food journal, I found that I had been avoiding my anger through this pattern of behavior for many years. With this new information I was able to begin making a conscious decision to experience my anger as it surfaced instead of eating.

When I would find myself standing in front of the refrigerator, looking for something to eat, I would remind myself that this was a pattern I had used in the past to avoid my feeling of anger. Instead of eating I would call a friend or review my day to see what had evoked my anger.

Our eating patterns can provide us with the information we need to begin experiencing our feelings and resolving those issues we have yet to address. A great deal of courage and honesty are needed to look at these patterns and behavior. Once we risk looking at our patterns, we soon discover they are the keys that unlock the door to feelings and unresolved issues long in need of our attention. With this door unlocked, we are firmly on the path toward self-discovery and growth.

10

What I Have Discovered About My Eating Disorder

Complete the following questions about your eating disorder.

1. The feelings I avoid as a result of my eating disorder are _____
   _____
   _____

2. I avoid my feelings by obsessing on food and my body or exercising in the following ways _____
   _____
   _____
   _____

3. I am most prone to my eating disorder during the following stressful situations (listing four examples) _____
   _____
   _____
   _____
   _____

4. My eating disorder appears to be difficult during these specific times of the day (listing times and giving three examples) _____
_____
_____
_____

5. When I am around friends, my eating disorder _____
_____
_____

6. When I am around my family, my eating disorder _____
_____
_____
_____

7. When I am at work or school, my eating disorder _____
_____
_____
_____

8. When I am with a member of the opposite sex, my eating disorder
_____
_____
_____

9. When I am under pressure or approaching a deadline, my eating disorder _____
_____
_____

10. When I have sex, my eating disorder _____
_____
_____

11. When I have made a mistake or feel like a failure, my eating disorder
_____
_____

12. When I feel alone, ignored or abandoned, my eating disorder _____
_____
_____
_____

13. When I get into my eating disorder, afterwards I usually feel _____
_____
_____

14. How has my eating disorder affected me financially (cost of food, exercise equipment, clothes as a result of fluctuating weight, illness, sprains or injuries as a result of excessive exercising, loss of work, etc.)? (listing three examples) _____

_____

_____

_____

15. How has my eating disorder affected my health such as feeling fatigue and sluggishness, tooth decay, stomach problems, excessive illness, difficulty with menstrual cycle, skin rashes and breaking out, loss of hair or hair in poor condition, sleeping difficulties, light-headedness, dizziness, difficulty staying on track or focusing, etc.? (listing five examples) _____

_____

_____

_____

_____

16. How has my eating disorder affected my job or school performance? (listing three examples) _____

_____

_____

17. How has my eating disorder affected my relationship with my family? (listing three examples) _____

_____

_____

18. How has my eating disorder affected my relationship with friends and my ability to be honest in intimate relationships? (listing two examples) _____

_____

_____

19. How do I feel about myself as a result of having an eating disorder, and how has this disease affected my self-esteem? _____

_____

_____

20. I have avoided dealing with my eating disorder by (listing five examples) _____

_____

_____

_____

_____

I promise myself that I will not allow the above behaviors or situations to interfere with my recovery from my addiction. I am committed to taking responsibility for my disease because I am the most important person in my life. This is my commitment to me.

_____   _____

Name   *Date*

You have just made one of the most important commitments you will ever make in your life! You have made a pledge to begin learning how to love yourself! **Congratulations!!!**

11

Eating Patterns And Behavior

Take some time to review your food journal and the 20 questions you have just completed. See if you can begin to understand how your eating patterns and behavior work. You may have to review your written material several times before you can clearly see your patterns of behavior. As you start to determine what feelings your behaviors have enabled you to avoid, begin writing them. They will become clearer as you list them. Try to list at least three patterns of behavior and give several examples for each pattern.

1. _____
   _____
   _____
   _____
   _____
   _____

2. _____
   _____
   _____

3. _____

12

Feelings: A True Adventure

During my early recovery from the disease of chemical dependency and bulimia, people asked me what I was feeling. I didn't understand what they meant. I had used chemicals and food for many years to cover up or avoid how I was feeling. While involved in my addictions, I wanted to be void of any feeling; feelings scared me, and I didn't know how to deal with them. I thought my feelings were the enemy and treated them as such.

Over a period of time, more and more of my feelings began surfacing as a result of abstaining from chemicals and addictive behavior with food. I became terrified. Half of the time I didn't even know what I was feeling. One day I would cry for no apparent reason, only to find myself sitting in total, all-encompassing fear the following day. My anger scared me, and my sadness, which would appear so suddenly, seemed to last forever. I felt confused because I thought that when I entered recovery, life would be wonderful. I was feeling overwhelmed and imprisoned by my feelings.

Eventually my life did improve. I began to see that in order for me to learn how to live with my feelings, my attitude toward them needed to change. The more I ran from my feelings the more powerful they became. I knew

69

I couldn't bury them with chemicals and food as I had in the past; instead I learned how to face them. It was as if my feelings were begging for my attention, demanding that I not neglect them any longer. As I became willing to experience my feelings of anger, pain, shame, joy, sadness, fear, numbness and others, I discovered that they could guide me through the healing process and promote growth. I became less intimidated by my feelings as I continued to work with them. Today they are my most precious companions.

13

Shame

For many of us the thought of allowing ourselves our anger, sadness, pain, fear, shame or even joy initiate strong old thought patterns from within that say, "It's not okay to feel that way," "Pull yourself together and be strong," "Stop crying," "If you're going to act like that go to your room," "Don't be a cry baby," and "Keep your feelings to yourself; don't wear them on your shirt sleeves." The shame that we begin to feel when we attempt to do feeling work can sabotage our efforts.

First, we may have to allow the shame we carry about to come to the surface. This is not a pleasant experience, but it is important that we begin allowing ourselves to feel shame in small doses. While facing shame we should also have support from recovery groups and friends or a therapist. By allowing shame to surface, we take away some of the power it has over us. Shame can disguise itself as: (1) a sick feeling in our stomachs ("icky" and "disgusting" are adjectives that can aid in describing how our stomachs feel) or (2) feelings of isolation, of aloneness and of being a human mistake.

Any time we are abused emotionally, physically or sexually as a child or as an adult, we feel shame about who we are. When someone abuses us, we are being shamed and discounted as human beings. To be told that it is not acceptable to have certain feelings is abusive and shaming. When we are shamed about our feelings, our emotional growth comes to a halt because we are not able to process, experience and work through the healing process.

Many of us enter addiction as a result of the shame we feel. We are lacking the healthy tools necessary for working with shame and discover that addiction can temporarily relieve us from this unpleasant feeling. The major problem with this method of shame reduction is that the consequences we suffer as a result of addiction eventually outweigh any relief we had previously experienced. Also, we begin to discover that as we continue in addictive behavior, the shame we have as a result of this compounds our problem even further. Then not only do we bear the initial shame addiction previously covered up, but also we carry shame about having the addiction itself. Thus, when we get into recovery, it is necessary to face our shame about our addiction and determine where our shame originated. First, let's look at how we perceive shame.

Perception Of Shame

Complete the following 23 questions.

1. If you could give the shame you have about your eating disorder physical form, what would it look like? Describe its size and color.

_____

_____

_____

_____

_____

2. If you would like, draw it and give the shame color with colored markers or pencils.

3. Also, if you could give it different names, besides shame, what would those names be?

_____

_____

_____
_____
_____
_____

4. Sometimes we can feel our shame inside our bodies. For some of us, it lives in our stomach or chest area; for others, it seems to cover us from head to toe. Close your eyes and try to get a general idea of where your shame is and then write about it. _____
_____
_____
_____

5. Somtimes it is helpful for us to write a letter to our shame. We need to let it know how we feel about having an eating disorder. Or we may want to write it an eviction notice, letting it know we are ready to evict if from its current residency. Write a letter to your shame; then close your eyes and imagine what your shame looks like. Now, in your mind's eye, hand the letter you have written to your shame. Describe this experience. _____
_____
_____
_____

6. How did it feel to confront your shame? Describe your feelings. _____
_____
_____
_____

7. If you have been emotionally, physically or sexually abused, close your eyes and try to imagine what your shame looks like in relation to those issues. Describe this shame. _____
_____
_____
_____

8. Draw this shame.

9. Write this shame a short note, letting it know that you are aware if its presence and that in the future you will be addressing it in greater detail.

_____

_____

_____

_____

_____

_____

_____

10. Close your eyes and visualize your face and body. Can you describe what you see in your mind's eye? _____

_____

_____

_____

_____

_____

_____

11. If you could rate your physical appearance as you see it from one to ten (with one being unacceptable and ten being exceptional), where would you place yourself? _____

_____

_____

In general, when we are carrying a lot of shame about our bodies, we tend to be more critical of ourselves.

12. Go look at yourself in a mirror and then describe what you see. _____

_____

_____

_____

_____

13. Did you focus more on those things you dislike about yourself than you did on those things you like about yourself? _____

_____

_____

14. Ask a friend or family member to describe to you how each perceives you physically, emotionally and intellectually, and then write the description. _____

_____

_____

_____
_____
_____
_____

15. Compare the description in 14 with descriptions you have written in 10, 11 and 12.

16. How does your description of yourself compare with that of your friend's or family member's description? _____
_____
_____
_____
_____

17. List ten things you dislike about yourself.

1. _____   6. _____
2. _____   7. _____
3. _____   8. _____
4. _____   9. _____
5. _____   10. _____

18. List ten things you like about yourself.

1. _____   6. _____
2. _____   7. _____
3. _____   8. _____
4. _____   9. _____
5. _____   10. _____

19. Which of the above lists was easier to do, 17 or 18? _____
Why? _____
_____
_____
_____
_____

20. Where do you feel you learned to be so critical of yourself, or who taught you to be so critical of yourself? _____
_____
_____
_____
_____

21. If you could pick one compliment you would most like to hear about your physical appearance, what would it be? _____

_____
_____
_____

22. If you could pick one compliment you would most like to hear from your parents, what would that be? _____
   _____
   _____
   _____

23. Write the two compliments together on three separate pieces of paper. Put one on your bathroom mirror, another on the dashboard of your car and place the last one in your wallet, purse or pocket. When you see them, read them aloud to yourself.

   Congratulations!!! You have taken a giant step toward confronting your shame.

14

Anger

Early in my recovery a woman said to me, "Carla, you have a great deal of anger, and some day you are going to have to address it." I did not understand what she was talking about for quite some time. As far as I was concerned, I didn't have an issue with anger. I decided this woman didn't know what she was talking about.

Sometime later, I began to feel overwhelmed with this powerful feeling. Initially I was scared because I feared it would overtake me and I would lose all control. The first time I allowed my anger to surface in recovery was before I was to have a small dinner party. I remember being angry that my plans for this gathering were not proceeding as planned. My anger about the situation had been building during the day, and it finally emerged early in the evening just before my guests were to arrive. I remember saying, "All right, I give up. This just isn't working and I'm really angry!" All day long I had been trying to control my anger by discounting it, feeling trapped and frustrated and wanting to binge. I finally acknowledged my anger and gave up control. As I did this I felt a renewed sense of power. I was able to use this power to take action and reevaluate the situation. After reassessing my plans for the evening, I was able to make the changes necessary to run the party smoothly.

With this experience and others like it, I began to see that the woman who had confronted me about my anger was right. I did have to deal with a great amount of anger. I hadn't experienced healthy anger in many years and saw that my addictions had only prolonged and masked the anger work I really needed to do. With this realization, I proceeded to write a list of the past and present issues about which I had anger. I remember asking several friends how long I would have this anger, and the reply was, "For as long as you need to."

Power From Anger

Our anger can provide for us the power necessary to review those past and present issues that are still in need of resolution. This power also can provide us with the courage that is necessary for risking new behavior and experiencing life from a whole new perspective. For some of us, it is necessary to seek out the safety a therapist can provide. A therapist or therapy group can provide us with direction, support and validation while we do our anger work. It is essential that we allow our anger to surface because if we continue to stuff it or discount it, eventually our anger will display itself in unhealthy ways. Also, if we do not address our anger directly, there is a chance that we will misdirect it and find ourselves being angry with the wrong situation or person. With unresolved issues or unfinished business there is a tendency to misdirect the anger we still carry. For this reason, we should review all past and present resentments.

As mentioned earlier, many of us fear our anger. We carry with us the old tapes from our childhoods that say, "It's not okay to be angry," or "If you cannot say anything nice, don't say anything at all." We learn at a very early age if we experience or express anger, we are being naughty, mean, unkind, selfish, disrespectful or unacceptable. Many of us have been punished, abandoned or discounted as a result of having normal and natural angry feelings. A number of us may have grown up witnessing family members display anger and rage in inappropriate, unhealthy ways, such as through violence, physical abuse or explosiveness. We may have grown up fearing that if we expressed our anger we would behave as they did. As a result we may have chosen to avoid our anger altogether because we were never given healthy tools for working with it. We must review how we developed our concepts about anger before we can begin to feel comfortable with this feeling.

Reviewing Your Concepts Of Anger

Complete these questions about **anger**.

1. Do you remember ever feeling angry as a child? _____
   Describe the incident or incidents. _____
   _____
   _____
   _____

2. Was anger something that was seen as bad or unacceptable in your
   family of origin? _____
   How did you get that message? _____
   _____
   _____

   From whom did you get that message? _____
   _____
   _____

3. How was anger expressed in your family of origin by:
   Dad _____
   Mom _____
   Brothers _____
   Sisters _____
   Grandparents _____

4. Was there ever any violence in your family of origin, such as physical
   abuse, hitting or inappropriate raging? Or did you ever witness any
   family violence? To witness abusive behavior is abusive. Describe
   incidents, if any.
   _____
   _____
   _____

5. Were you ever punished for expressing anger? _____
   How and by whom? _____

   Describe the incident or incidents. _____
   _____
   _____
   _____
   _____

6. Many of us learn to stuff our anger by not feeling anger. This is a survival technique. We stuff or avoid our anger by eating, using chemicals, daydreaming, sleeping, tuning out emotionally, working or excelling in school. We may have misdirected our anger and begun fighting at school, with our spouses, our boss or others we care about as a result of discounting what it is we are feeling. You may know of other ways in which you have avoided your anger. List the ways you have avoided your anger and give examples.

1. _____

    _____

2. _____

    _____

3. _____

    _____

7. For many of us our anger may be disguised in the form of headaches, ulcers, feeling irritated or discontented with life. We may be accident prone, attributing our self-destructive behavior to clumsiness and lack of awareness. Some of us may find that we are quick tempered with those close to us. Our anger also may be disguised as depression, which can be a form of anger turned inward. It is important that we begin to see how our anger disguises itself. How do you think your anger disguises itself? List and give examples of this.

1. _____

    _____

2. _____

    _____

3. _____

    _____

8. Some of us are afraid of our anger. We fear we will lose all control. A few of us may even fear hurting ourselves or others. If you are fearful of your anger, describe below the worst possible consequences that could result from experiencing your anger. _____

    _____

    _____

    _____

9. Realistically, do you believe the above could happen? _____

    _____

Some of us may find that our fears are not realistic while others may have fears that are very real. For those of us who see that our fears are not realistic but instead the result of old tapes from childhood, it is important that we begin addressing these tapes. List those tapes that are keeping you from experiencing your anger.

1. _____

_____

2. _____

_____

3. _____

_____

10. Now, rewrite each of the preceding old tapes, incorporating the positive aspects of allowing yourself to affirm your anger. For example, "I have a right to my anger," "Anger is a healthy, natural feeling," or "My anger is a healing feeling and therefore necessary for my growth."

1. _____

_____

2. _____

_____

3. _____

_____

Dealing With Fear Of Anger

There are those of us who do have realistic concerns that support our fear of anger. Some of us have suffered serious consequences as a result of acting out rage. We may have hurt someone else, ourselves or damaged property. Raging such as this produces shame for us and can keep us from learning how to experience anger in a healthy way. Raging is usually the result of childhood emotional, physical or sexual abuse, and treatment or therapy is strongly recommended.

For those of us who do suffer from this type of raging behavior or *rageaholism,* it is crucial that we see how this behavior is interfering with our recovery. When we rage, we feel shame about our behavior and then stuff our anger. As we continue to stuff our anger we are building up to rage. Eventually we reach a point where we can no longer stuff our anger and we lose control. The anger we have stuffed comes out as rage all at one time, and we feel as if we have just exploded. After we explode, we feel shame about our behavior and may cover up the shame with food, drugs, alcohol or some mood-altering behavior. We find that we are caught in a vicious cycle of self-destructive behavior. For this reason, we may need assistance in breaking the cycle.

For raging behavior, such as this, it is necessary to learn how to deal with our anger as it emerges. Healthy anger empowers us and allows for changes, whereas out-of-control raging results in feeling shame. If you do rage, list examples of this and also include the consequences of such behavior.

1. Example: lost control and raged. Threw dishes. Consequence: broke a favorite dish.

2. _____
   _____

3. _____
   _____

4. _____
   _____

5. _____
   _____

Keeping A Rage Journal

If you do rage, it will be helpful to begin keeping a rage journal. This journal can provide information about those situations that trigger or set off raging behavior. Follow the guidelines used for the food journal. Also, you may want to seek out therapeutic assistance. It is important that you have a safe environment in which to address this issue because it usually involves shame and abuse. It is possible to change this behavior. It takes a lot of courage to address this most painful issue, and I support those of you who do follow through in seeking assistance.

We can learn how to have healthy anger if we are open to experiencing new ways of behaving. Our anger can become a tool of healing. Many of us carry anger about past abuse and unresolved family-of-origin issues. We continue to carry this unfinished business until we are willing to address it and heal. Until then it only interferes with our growth process. For a number of us, our anger or rage covers up our pain and old hurt. To be able to heal, we must first reach our pain. This is why it is necessary for us to experience our anger as it surfaces. Also, our anger empowers us with the ability to take action and make change, bringing us many gifts as we experience it.

15

Fear

Fear is learned. If one touches a hot stove over and over again, eventually one will learn that a hot stove can cause burns. Have you ever noticed that small children are afraid of those things their parents fear? If mother fears lightning and hides under her bed covers during electrical storms, her children will quickly learn that storms are something to fear.

For example, when my son was a year old, I became very aware of how closely he was observing my responses and reactions to everyday situations. I also noticed that he mimicked a number of my behaviors. This copying behavior is normal for young children and a part of the developmental process. But, it is this normal process that can set us up for unhealthy fears. I realized what an impact learned fear had when my child was learning how to walk. Every time he would stumble, he would look at me to see how I was reacting. If I were visibly upset, he would begin to cry even though he had not been hurt. If my reaction were one of encouragement, he would get right back up and be on his merry way.

Fear is a learned response that is passed down from one generation to another. Some fear is healthy and necessary because it enables us to protect ourselves. By learning that a hot stove can burn, we also learn that we can protect our fingers by not touching a hot stove. Healthy fear can provide us with the strength and courage we need to care for ourselves. In this way our fear can be a teacher. But, many of us carry a great deal of learned fear that can keep us from risking new behavior and exploring life.

For some of us our fears can be paralyzing. We may be aware on an intellectual level that some of our fears are illogical and without reason. On a feeling level our fears can seem overwhelming and be very real. Many of us end up shaming ourselves for our fears, discounting once again that feelings are either right or wrong. We lose an opportunity for growth when we discount our fears. Because we are willing to grow, let's take a close look at *fear*.

Many of us have difficulty in understanding when we are experiencing fear. Others may experience the feeling of fear as a strong need to run and hide. Or we may have heart palpitations that feel so strong we fear our heart will jump out of our chest. Possibly we perspire more than usual and feel as though we are going to lose all control of our bodily functions. Feeling anxious or experiencing panic attacks may completely immobilize us. Some of us may become isolated and not answer the telephone or doorbell. A few of us may hide under our bed covers fearful of what is "out there."

Many of us may begin to compulsively eat. We may find ourselves eating without thinking about it. Before we know it, we have eaten through the contents of our pantries and refrigerators. The shame we feel after we have binged temporarily moves us away from our fear. Eventually the same fear will return, and if we cover it up, we will never resolve it or learn from it.

Experiencing Fear

It is important for us to understand how we experience fear. What does our fear look like? If we are unsure of what our fear looks like, we can begin by guessing.

1. List five ways you feel you experience fear or what you think happens to you when you are fearful of someone or something.

   1. _____
   2. _____
   3. _____
   4. _____
   5. _____

For the majority of us, our fear is learned as a result of growing up in our family of origin. Some fear is necessary and healthy. But when fear is overwhelming, it can be unhealthy. For example, I had an overwhelming fear of fat. I would be weight appropriate and find myself overwhelmed with a fear of fat. Or, if I had put on a couple of pounds, my fear about fat would disrupt and affect every area of my life. It was as if my emotion, being, ability to function, manner of dress and behavior were totally dictated by fearing what the bathroom scale would say. During these times, those around me would point out how illogical my fear was. I would become confused and feel shame about my fears because to me they seemed so real.

Types of Fear

Some of the other **fears** we can have follow:

1. Being out of control
2. Being alone
3. Being with people
4. Feelings such as anger, sadness, grief
5. Being weak
6. Success
7. Economical insecurity
8. Having security
9. Not being accepted
10. Women
11. Men
12. Aging
13. Responsibility
14. Being assertive
15. Intimacy and getting too close
16. Trusting
17. Loss
18. Driving automobiles
19. Open spaces
20. Flying
21. Dirt and germs
22. Animals
23. Cultural differences
24. Not being right
25. Failure
26. Being trapped
27. The dark
28. Heights
29. God
30. Death

These are just a few of the fears we may carry with us. Everyone is different, and it is important that we begin taking an honest look at our fears.

Examining Fears

With a blue pen list as many of your fears as you can and try to list them objectively without judgment.

1.
2.
3.
4.
5.
6.
7.
8.
9.
10.
11.
12.
13.
14.
15.
16.
17.
18.
19.
20.

Now go back and list whether or not there is an explanation for each fear. For some there may not be an explanation; whereas, for others there may be many. Write your explanations next to your fears in black pen.

While doing family-of-origin work, I began to see that many of the fears I carried were similar to those fears my family members had. Some of them were healthy fears that protected me. However, others were confusing and caused difficulty for me. I needed to look at those fears my family members carried.

List the fears you feel your mother has in blue pen.

    1.
    2.
    3.
    4.
    5.
    6.
    7.
    8.
    9.
   10.

List the fears you feel your father has in blue pen.

    1.
    2.
    3.
    4.
    5.
    6.
    7.
    8.
    9.
   10.

Some of you may feel the two above exercises are difficult. Guess if necessary. Our guesses tend to be close to reality.

If you have brothers and sisters, list what you feel are their fears in blue pen.

Brother

    1.
    2.
    3.
    4.
    5.
    6.
    7.
    8.
    9.
   10.

Sister

    1.
    2.
    3.
    4.
    5.
    6.
    7.
    8.
    9.
    10.

Take the list of your mother's fears, your father's fears, your brother's or sister's fears and compare them with your fears. Use a red pen to circle the fears you and your family members have in common. List these fears.

    1.
    2.
    3.
    4.
    5.
    6.
    7.
    8.
    9.
    10.

Place a black check next to those fears you feel are necessary and healthy. List the fears that appear to be overwhelming and difficult for you.

    1.
    2.
    3.
    4.
    5.

If you know or would have to guess, where do these fears come from? Did you learn them from your family of origin and if so, who taught them to you? Or, are they the result of a painful or traumatic experience? Spend time writing three or four sentences for each fear telling where you believe it originated. Also, write about the ways it is causing you difficulty today.

Having an idea of where our fears come from allows us to work with them and learn from them. We can discover more about ourselves and our family of origin by facing our fears. If we are willing to face our fears, especially those that are interfering with our growth process, we can reclaim some of the power they have over us. Continuing to talk and to write about our fears makes it possible for us to use them to our advantage.

If confronted with unhealthy, overwhelming fear, we can use the opportunity to discover where the fear comes from; on the other hand our healthy fears can force us to take action to protect and care for ourselves. Some of our fears can guide us toward new avenues of growth. Because of this, it is important for us to determine what our fears are and where they come from. Once we can do this, we are free to choose how to use the information they have provided. Then we can decide what we want to do with our fears.

As we confront our fears, they slowly lose the power they have over us. Ultimately, we can choose to keep those fears that protect us and resolve the fears that prevent us from growing.

16

Grief, Sadness And Spirituality

When I was 16 years old, my mother died of cancer. Because I did not know how to talk about my loss or feel my grief, I found that food and alcohol allowed me to survive that painful period of my life. As a result of my addictions, I was never able to resolve the loss of my mother. The addictions that had enabled my survival kept me from healing.

I was not able to move through the grief process in a healthy manner because I had never learned how to have my feelings. My addictions were a temporary fix for the well of sadness I carried. When I began my recovery and gave up my addictions to food and alcohol, the grief surrounding my mother's death was still there. I had to learn how to move through the grief process and feel my feelings in order to heal.

Most of us have difficulty with sadness. I believe that our society as a whole does not know how to grieve loss. In some cultures, when there is a death, it is acceptable to grieve and even be encouraged by the surrounding community. The Jewish culture, for example, has a grieving period for the death of a loved one that lasts for one year. During this one-year period family members recite a blessing called the mourner's kaddish at worship services. The mourners are supported throughout the year in this process by their community. The grave of the loved one remains unmarked during the one-year period of mourning, after which a tombstone is placed on the grave during a religious ceremony called an "unveiling." This ceremony signifies that the year-long period of grieving is ended.

We not only need to grieve loss as a result of death, but also we need to grieve each time we experience loss, be it a job change, a geographical move or the end of a relationship. We need to have our sadness about our losses in order to heal from them. If we do not heal from loss, we continue to carry it with us throughout our lives. This failure to heal keeps us from growing and experiencing life.

For many of us, food was our best friend and a source of comfort. As a result of our recovery from food addiction, we find we have to grieve the loss of our dysfunctional relationship with food. This is similar to the recovering alcoholic finally having to grieve his lost relationship with alcohol. We need to grieve our food addiction because it did allow us to survive many of life's problems. It protected us from those feelings we feared and it insulated us from our pain. Even though our food addiction was destructive and dysfunctional, it is important to remember that it did enable us to survive. The healthy tools that are necessary for working through life problems weren't available to us.

For those of us who come from families where certain feelings were not allowed, we will find we do not know how to grieve. As we begin to recover from our addiction to food, we will find we have a number of grief issues and losses that never have been resolved. We may begin to have feelings about issues we once thought were long forgotten. As we experience these feelings, they may seem overwhelming. Whenever we experience strong feelings about past or present losses, it is significant to realize we still carry unresolved grief about those losses. Once we identify what our sadness is about, we can begin the process of healing.

There are a number of stages we need to work through within the grief process. These stages are *denial, shock, bargaining, anger, sorrow/sadness, depression,* and finally *spirituality, acceptance* and *forgiveness.* We move through them at our own individual pace, and each of our experiences with this process is a little different.

As we will soon see, it is necessary for us to move through each of these stages every time we experience loss. If we do not do this, we cannot heal from the pain of loss. For example, if a relationship comes to an end as a result of divorce, both parties must grieve the loss of the relationship. If they grieve, they will be able to have their feelings and resolve those issues that caused them pain while in the relationship. Also, while they grieve their loss, they will be able to learn and grow. They will gain insight into themselves and the relationship. If they do not grieve, they will carry with them into the next relationship all of the unresolved feelings and issues of this relationship.

Different Stages Of The Grieving Process

Since it is vital for us to learn how to grieve, let's look at the different stages involved in the grieving process.

Denial

As mentioned earlier, the first stage of the grief process is denial. We have difficulty believing the loss has actually taken place. We feel that the loss really hasn't affected us. We have a difficult time accepting what has happened. We may say, "Well, the relationship is over and I don't feel sad at all," "I gave up my eating disorder and it wasn't difficult at all — I feel fine," or "I left my job and am glad to be rid of it." We do not believe our loss has affected us. In some cases we are so relieved at not having the relationship, the addiction or the job that we enjoy our new found freedom for awhile. For example, with a death we may feel as though the departed loved one is only on a long vacation, and we deny how final death really is.

Shock

Eventually, we realize that our loss is very real and enter a stage of feeling shocked. We think, "The relationship really is over," "My eating disorder really has been very self-destructive," or "I'm not going to be working in that office or with those same people again." We begin to discover that our loss does have an effect on us. With the death of a loved one, family members begin to feel the loved one's absence and realize that this is final. The death begins to feel very real, where before it may have seemed like a dream.

Bargaining

We may find ourselves bargaining with our loss, ourselves or even with our Higher Power, not wanting to accept totally the impact our loss has had on us. We tell ourselves, "Well, I will see her on some occasion, so the relationship isn't really over," "I'll be able to binge sometimes. I can't give up my eating disorder totally; I need something to fall back on," or "Maybe I'll be working at that office again. Who knows, I may end up working on a project with my new company and my old company together in the future." We find ourselves not accepting that people, things and situations change. With the death of a loved one, we may find ourselves bargaining with our Higher Power. We may have difficulty packing up the belongings and clothes of our loved ones, still hoping that someday they will return.

Anger

After we have bargained over our loss for awhile, we find ourselves becoming angry. We find ourselves being angry with everyone around us and life in general. We begin to realize that we are angry about our loss: "I'm really angry that she left me. How could she after all I have done for her?" "Why do I have to have this damn eating disorder? This isn't fair. Why me?" or "They don't even care that I'm gone from that office. This shows me how little they really appreciated me." Some of us may find ourselves experiencing anger toward our loss and our Higher Power about our loss. At the death of a loved one, family members may begin feeling feelings of resentment about being abandoned. Nevertheless, it is vital for us to have anger about our losses.

Sorrow And Sadness

Eventually, after we have spent a great deal of time moving back and forth through the stages of denial, shock, bargaining and anger, we begin to experience deep sorrow. Our loss really does hurt. We feel empty, alone and depressed. For many, the grief process comes to a halt at this point. The sadness that accompanies this phase of the grief process can seem overwhelming. We may find ourselves looking for ways to cover up our pain. It is significant to know that these feelings are normal for this stage in the grief process. Our sadness is necessary for our healing, and to cover up our pain at this point is self-defeating. We may find that we do not want to get out of bed in the morning because we feel life has no purpose. We feel lethargic and experience waves of crying. One minute we can feel fine only to suddenly experience intense sadness the next moment, sobbing uncontrollably.

Depression

We also can experience a general depressive attitude toward life and feel a need to isolate ourselves. We may experience difficulty with sleep. We either want to sleep all the time or experience insomnia. Even our food can become a problem. We can have difficulty in eating at all or may find ourselves wanting to binge to cover up the pain.

Spirituality

Spiritually we may feel alone and have difficulty reaching out to others or a Higher Power. We may find ourselves questioning our faith and reevaluating our relationship with our Higher Power. This period of grieving can be a time for turning inward and experiencing who we are as spiritual beings. Then, too, it can be a time for spiritual growth. If we do not have a relationship with a Higher Power, the grief process can force us into exploring why we don't. Usually, when we have difficulty with a concept of a Higher Power, we have a great deal of unresolved issues around trust. Maybe our trust has been abused. We may still carry with us unresolved abuse issues from our family of origin. We still may have anger about our losses and find ourselves asking, "How could a Higher Power let this happen?"

Some of us may fear trusting a Higher Power. Our first concept of a Higher Power comes to us as children in the form of our parents. We attribute to our Higher Power many of the characteristics our parents possess. If we had difficulty trusting our mother or father, we probably will have difficulty trusting a Higher Power. If we feared our mother or father, we may fear a Higher Power.

If we experience difficulty with our Higher Power in our grief, we may want to make a list of the characteristics we feel our Higher Power has. For example, do we feel our Higher Power is kind, nonjudgmental and safe, or do we feel our Higher Power is judgmental, punishing and rigid? Next, we will want to make a list of all those characteristics we feel our parents have. Were our parents loving, caring, accepting, rejecting, rigid or undependable? Then, as we compare these lists with one another, we may begin to see that we may have to redefine our Higher Power or work toward removing Mom or Dad as our Higher Power.

For a time some of us may need to express anger toward our Higher Power about the pain and issues of grief we have in our lives. Then there will be those of us who feel very comfortable and safe with the Higher Power in our life. We feel secure in knowing that our Higher Power will see us through this painful period of growth. We have faith in knowing that we are not alone. Our grief can strengthen our relationship with our Higher Power as we move through this phase of the grieving process. Grief also can encourage us to develop the spiritual side of our being.

Acceptance

Eventually we will realize that we are beginning to feel good about life and who we are. We find ourselves feeling light and cheerful. We can finally say, "I feel sad about my loss, but it is time to move on," "Well, I do have an eating disorder and my addiction to food has really taught me a lot," or "I am sad about leaving my friends at my job. That job really taught me a lot." This stage of the grief process is called the acceptance phase. Here we are able to accept our loss as a part of the life process. We have allowed ourselves to feel all of our feelings about the loss, especially our feelings of anger and sadness. As a result of this, we have healed. We can accept ourselves for who we are and life for what it is. We feel stronger for having survived this process and have the courage to risk and participate in the here and now.

Forgiveness

Forgiveness evolves from acceptance. With acceptance we can forgive ourselves for being addicts, forgive those who have left us and feel confident in knowing our grief was necessary for our healing.

Where are you in the grief process and how do you feel about sadness and loss? For some, there may be fear in exploring this area of recovery. It is strongly suggested you have a support system you can feel safe with while working toward resolving grief issues. Let your support systems know you are working on these issues and ask for their support.

Grief Questionnaire

1. How do you know you are feeling sad? Do you cry, feel depressed, isolate yourself, eat less, sleep more, feel alone and abandoned, or do you begin to binge? List the ways you experience sadness. If you have difficulty with this exercise, think back on a time when you remember you were sad and list your behaviors. Give examples.

   _____

   _____

   _____

   _____

2. When we are sad, sometimes our bodies react. We may feel a heaviness or pain in our chest area; we may feel as though we are carrying the weight of the world on our shoulders or in our stomach area. And, we can feel dizzy and light-headed. Do you remember how your body felt? _____ If so, please list these experiences with examples.

   _____

   _____

   _____

We learn how to grieve and have our sadness by watching how our parents experience grief and sadness.

3. When my **mother** was sad, she would _____

   _____

4. When my **father** was sad, he would _____
   _____

5. When my **sister** was sad, she would _____
   _____

6. When my **brother** was sad, he would _____
   _____

7. When I was sad in my family as a child, I would _____
   _____

8. When I was sad as a child, my mother would _____
   _____

9. When I was sad as a child, my father would _____
   _____

Another good indicator of our ability to grieve revolves around the issues of death and how the topic of death was dealt with in our family of origin.

10. The first person I ever remember dying in my family was _____
    I felt _____

11. My mother seemed to feel _____

12. My father seemed to feel _____

13. Describe the events and behaviors you observed surrounding this death. For example, did your mother and father provide you with spiritual solutions to death, or was there a no-talk rule about death? Do you think your parents were able to see death as a part of the life process or were they fearful of death? _____
    _____
    _____
    _____

14. The first person to ever explain what death was to me was _____

15. Describe how death was first explained to you. _____
    _____

_____

_____

16. When death was explained to me for the first time, I remember feeling _____

Did you ever lose anyone as a result of death who was very close to you during your childhood? A parent, a grandparent, a brother, a sister, a friend or a pet?

17. If so, how do you remember feeling? _____

_____

18. How do you feel about that loss now? _____
Do you still need to grieve this loss? Do you still feel sad or angry about this loss? _____

19. Write about how you feel about this loss. _____

_____

_____

_____

_____

_____

Now review the stages of the grief process in order to determine whether or not you have completed the grieving process with this loss. Many of us have a difficult time with death because it forces us to confront our own mortality and spiritual relationship with our Higher Power.

20. How do you feel about your own mortality? _____

_____

_____

_____

_____

If this question seems difficult, it is because it forces us to reevaluate our spiritual beliefs. If you have difficulty with this question, you might want to explore your unresolved grief issues. As we work through these issues we can grow spiritually. Unresolved grief issues, along with those related to death, may include:

Losses we have experienced as a result of our eating disorder, such as —

- self-esteem
- time
- relationships and friends
- physical health
- money as a result of spending on our addiction
- spirituality and peace of mind
- trust in self and others
- life goals
- career goals
- emotional health

Losses we have experienced as a result of our dysfunctional family of origin, such as —

- our childhood
- support and nurturance
- our parents to addiction
- ability to play
- feeling protected and safe
- self-love and care
- privacy and boundaries
- ability to feel
- ability to trust
- ability to communicate in a healthy manner

21. List the losses you have experienced as a result of your eating disorder in black pen.

1.
2.
3.
4.
5.
6.
7.
8.
9.
10.

22. List any other losses you have experienced in your life in black pen.
    1.
    2.
    3.
    4.
    5.
    6.
    7.
    8.
    9.
    10.

23. Put a check in red pen next to each unresolved loss you still need to grieve.

    It is also important to review the religious beliefs we were brought up with when addressing grief, loss and sadness. Our Higher Power can be of great comfort during these times and our religious beliefs can influence how we feel about our Higher Power.

24. What religion did your mother participate in? _____

25. What religion did your father participate in? _____

26. In what religion were you raised by your family? _____

27. Did you like your religion? _____

28. If so, why? If not, why not? _____
    _____

29. What do you think your mother's concept of a Higher Power is like?
    _____

30. What do you think your father's concept of a Higher Power is like?
    _____
    Do you agree with their concept? _____

31. What is your concept of a Higher Power? _____
    _____

32. List what you like about your Higher Power. _____
_____

33. List what you dislike about your Higher Power, if anything. _____
_____

34. If you could change your concept of your Higher Power, what would
you change? _____
_____

You can make those changes!

I believe that knowing how to grieve and experience our sadness is one
of the most crucial aspects of recovery from addiction. So many of us fear
our sadness, and we push it away. Another priority in our healing is allowing
ourselves to feel sadness. It is our unresolved grief that leaves us feeling
empty within. We try to fill ourselves with food, drugs, alcohol, work,
relationships, sex, material goods and more, only to find our grief is still
there. When we permit ourselves to feel sadness, we begin to fill the
emptiness within. If we know how to grieve, we can truly learn how to live
life to the fullest. Grief and sadness are not the enemy. They are the feelings
that guide us along the path toward continued self-realization and growth.

17

Our Family Of Origin And Food

Before we complete our investigation of how we feel our feelings and why we do the things we do, let's explore our family of origin a bit further.

What Males And Females Are

Children learn about what males and females are by watching those males and females within their family system. If the females in the system have difficulty in knowing themselves, expressing feelings, trusting their own perceptions and loving themselves, the children will develop many mixed messages about what a female is.

This same idea holds true for those concepts developed by children about what a male is. If the men in the family system have difficulty in expressing emotion or in accepting themselves as creative and sensitive beings, the children in the system will have a limited perception of what a male is. Most of us live our lives accepting, without choice, those characteristics and beliefs about males and females we have been brought up with in our family of origin. For example, we may have heard "Men don't cry and women are emotional," or "Men are concrete and logical while women are intuitive and creative." Rigid generalizations such as these can rob us of the motivation that is necessary to further explore who we are.

Beliefs And Values

We also have received a number of beliefs and values from our family of origin about what food means and why we eat. Have you ever noticed that within different families behavior at dinnertime is unique for each of those systems? In one family dinnertime may be very businesslike. People in this family may not talk while eating, and having a meal together seems like work. They eat at exactly the same time every night, and the whole experience is completed within 15 minutes. This may be followed by rigid cleaning up, where everyone has an assigned task. In other families the dinner experience may be chaotic with dinnertime being very unpredictable. When this family does sit down to eat, all of the problems of that day and those unresolved from yesterday are discussed. People may argue and fight and, in some cases where violence is involved, food or plates fly across the room. Dinner in this family may last for several hours because nobody is allowed to leave the table until the latest crisis has been hashed over many times. Or, people may come and go during this dinner period, eating a little bit here and a little more there.

Requirements For Acceptance And Approval

Many of us have come from families where membership in the "Clean Plate Club" was necessary for acceptance and approval. Messages such as "You better clean your plate if you want dessert," or "Want to grow up big and strong?" are common in dysfunctional families. A favorite comment within dysfunctional families seems to be: "Eat all of your food. Do you know people are starving right now because they haven't any food?"

I know of an instance where a young boy, after hearing the above comment over and over, decided to take action. He felt so much shame about not wanting to finish his food that he began saving his leftovers. He put his leftovers in a shoebox and wrapped it up for mailing. He addressed it to "The Starving People Who Have No Food." Needless to say, the post office returned the smelly box of old food to the boy with a message that said, "Name one." Even though this story may seem funny, it is at the same time incredibly sad. This little boy felt shame about not finishing his plate, although he was full because his physical body was telling him to stop eating. He was receiving a message that something was wrong with him for not wanting to eat. These are the kinds of messages that cause us to grow into adults who do not trust our feelings and perceptions.

Intergenerational Patterns

Then, too, eating disorders may be *intergenerational.* Patterns of eating are passed from one generation to another. Addiction to trigger foods, such as sugar or white flour, also appear to be intergenerational and determined by one's genetic makeup.

The following is a scenario that describes how patterns of behavior can be passed from one generation to the next. Mother came from a dysfunctional family where her father was a workaholic and emotionally unavailable because he was rarely home. Her father had a great deal of difficulty expressing his feelings and feared intimacy. Her mother, who also came from a dysfunctional home, felt very lonely with her husband gone so much of the time but did not know how to express her feelings about this to him. She learned to cope with her sadness and loneliness with food and became overweight. Because both parents used addiction to avoid their difficulties, Mother never learned how to resolve life's problems in a healthy manner and grow through them. Thus, Mother grew into an adult who fears intimacy, has difficulty expressing her anger and does not know how to resolve life's problems in a healthy manner. As a result, she has difficulty in exploring who she is as a woman and in risking new experiences and behaviors.

As the daughter aged, she began to realize that she is a lot like her mother, and she may even have a weight problem like her mother or be obsessed with not gaining weight. She also may see that she has married a man just like her father, who is a workaholic and emotionally unavailable. Since she hasn't any intimacy with her husband, she fills herself with food, avoiding the feelings of shame, fear, loneliness and anger. Her daughter, watching all of this, swears to herself that she will not be overweight like her grandmother and mother. Also, she promises herself that she will marry a man who is home more often than her father was.

Committing herself to a seven-day exercise program, the daughter becomes obsessed with her weight. Eventually she marries a man who seems committed to her and appears to be a real homebody. Several years down the road, she finds herself overeating. She discovers she can control this by throwing up. Her husband has become very involved with his business and is rarely home. Her life is out of control, and she cannot understand how she ended up in this situation. Also, she is frustrated about her eating behavior and fears she will lose all control and be overweight.

Another situation may be as follows. Dad was raised in a family system where his father was a violent alcoholic. Whenever his father was intoxicated, he would become verbally and physically abusive. Living in this home was a frightening experience. His mother feared for her safety and had difficulty protecting her children from her husband's alcoholic rages. On many occasions Dad would end up protecting his mother from his father. After a night of terror, his mother would bake pies or cakes the following day. This was to make up to the children for her husband's behavior. Dad learned that he could avoid the chaos and fear in his family of origin by eating. With food he could nurture himself and cover up the shame he felt about being abused by his father.

As he grew into young adulthood, he continued this process of stuffing his feelings with food. When he felt angry feelings or was confronted with the angry feelings of others, he would find himself at the doughnut shop. He never learned that there was a difference between anger and rage. He fears that he will rage as his father did if he allows himself his angry feelings.

In time he marries a woman who has difficulty being responsible for herself. She is very needy and has a number of physical complaints. She is addicted to several prescription medications and complains about her many fears. Though he feels it is his job to protect her, he is frustrated with her for not exploring life and taking risks on her own. Out of anger toward her, combined with all of the old hurts from the past, he finds himself as an adult nurturing himself with food as he did during his childhood.

His son, observing all of this, finds that he doesn't know how to express anger in a healthy way. He rages, starts fights at school and throws things. When he rages, he feels out of control and shameful. He knows that it is not acceptable to be angry in his family because his parents never act angry. But he doesn't know what to do and fears his own violent behavior. He learns that he can forget about this problem and others by going out with his friends and having a couple of beers. And so it goes as the cycle continues from one generation to another.

These situations are common. Many of us carry beliefs and behavior patterns that are several generations old. We learned some of them from our mothers and others from our fathers. We may be aware of some of them and not as aware of others. Many of these patterns are so deeply rooted within us that we are powerless over them. Because we are unaware of many of them, it is important for our recovery that we begin asking a few simple questions about our family of origin. Hopefully, these questions will fill in the missing blanks and enable us to see our own behavior patterns more clearly.

Parental Patterns

So that we may understand our own patterns of behavior better, answer the following questions about patterns our parents had.

Dad

1. How did Dad look physically? _____
_____

2. Did he like how he looked physically? _____
Was he concerned about how he dressed? _____
Who bought his clothes? _____

3. Was Dad overweight? _____ Underweight? _____
How did Dad feel about gaining too much weight? Or how did Dad feel about other people gaining too much weight? _____
_____

What kind of comments, if any, did he make about overweight or underweight people? _____
_____

4. How did Dad show concern about his physical health? _____
_____

Did he smoke? ____ Did he drink? ____ Did he exercise? _____
Was he concerned about what he ate? _____

5. What do you think your dad thought it was to be male? _____
_____

Did he believe men were different from women? _____ How? _____
_____

6. Was your dad comfortable with his feelings? _____ How many times can you remember him crying? _____ Did he seem comfortable crying or was he embarrassed? _____

7. Did your dad feel comfortable around others feeling their feelings? ____
What would he do when someone near to him was crying? _____
_____ Angry? _____ Fearful? _____

8. How did your dad show his love for you and for others? _____ .
_____

9. How did your dad act at the dinner table? _____

10. Did your dad ever accuse you of being fat or make fun of you or your body in any way? _____ If so, how? _____
_____

11. Does your dad have any addictions you are aware of such as alcoholism, workaholism, drug addiction, food addictions, rageaholism, sexual addiction, addiction to religion, co-dependency? _____
_____

12. What information do you have about your dad's father? Did he have any addictions or do you suspect any? _____

13. Do you know what your dad's father looked like? If not, try to locate a photograph. Describe his physical characteristics. Was he overweight? Underweight? _____
_____

14. If you know or knew this grandfather, how did he show his love to you, your dad and others? _____
Did he hug? _____ Did you like him? If so, why or if not, why?
_____
_____

15. What do you know about your dad's mother? _____
Did she have any addictions you are aware of? _____
_____

16. What did your dad's mother look like physically? If you don't know, try to locate a photograph. Describe her physical characteristics. Was she overweight? Underweight? _____
_____

17. If you know or knew this grandmother, how did she show her love to you, your dad and others? _____ Did she hug? _____
Did you like her? If so, why or if not, why? _____
_____

18. Do you believe your dad fully appreciates and loves himself as a male?
_____
_____

Mom

19. How did Mom look physically? _____
_____

20. Did she like how she looked physically? _____
Was she concerned about how she dressed? _____
Was she concerned about her hair? _____ Did she wear makeup? _____
How much? _____

21. Was Mom overweight or underweight? _____ How did Mom feel about gaining too much weight? Or, how did she feel about other people gaining too much weight? _____
_____

What kind of comments, if any, did she make about overweight people?
_____
_____
_____

22. How did Mom show concern about her physical health? _____
_____

Did she smoke? _____ Did she drink? _____ Did she exercise? _____
Was she concerned about what she ate? _____
_____

23. What do you feel your mom thought it was to be female? _____

Did she believe women and men were different and if so, how? _____
_____

24. Was your mom comfortable with her feelings? _____
How many times can you remember her crying? _____
Did she seem comfortable crying or was she embarrassed? _____

25. Did your mom feel comfortable around others feeling their feelings?
_____ What would she do when someone near to her was crying?
_____

Angry? _____ Fearful? _____
26. How did your mom act at the dinner table? _____
_____

27. Did your mom ever accuse you of being fat or make fun of you or your
body in any way? _____ If so, how? _____
_____

28. Does your mom have any addictions you are aware of such as
workaholism, alcoholism, drug addiction, rageaholism, food addiction,
addiction to religion, co-dependency or sexual addiction? _____
_____

29. Do you know what your mom's father looked like? If not, try to locate a
photograph. Describe his physical characteristics. Was he overweight or
underweight? _____
_____

30. If you know or knew this grandfather, how did he show his love to you,
your mom and others? _____
Did he hug? _____ Did you like him? _____
If so, why or if not, why? _____
_____

31. What do you know about your mom's mother? _____

    _____

    Did she have any addictions you are aware of? _____

32. What did your mom's mother look like physically? If you don't know, try
    to locate a photograph. Describe her physical characteristics. Was she
    overweight? Underweight? _____

    _____

33. If you know or knew this grandmother, how did she show her love to
    you, your mom and others? _____
    Did she hug? _____ Did you like her? If so, why or if not, why? _____

    _____

34. Do you believe your mom fully appreciates and loves herself as a
    female? _____

    _____

35. Do you know if either of your parents were ever abused emotionally,
    physically or sexually? _____

36. Are your parents still married, divorced or has either parent died? _____
    If divorced, do you know why? _____
    If one or both have died, what was the cause of death? _____

37. How did your parents display affection toward one another? _____

    _____

    _____

38. Who explained sex to you, Mom and Dad, Mom, Dad, or did you receive
    your information elsewhere? _____
    Did your parents seem comfortable with the topic of sex? _____
    Do you feel you were given enough information? _____
    Was it a pleasant or unpleasant experience? _____

39. How is your relationship with your parents now? Is it strained and
    difficult or is it comfortable and safe? _____

    _____

    Can you share with them openly and honestly, or is it difficult to
    communicate with them? _____

40. Which parent are you the closest to? _____ Why? _____

    _____

It is hopeful these questions have provided a new perspective for us on
our family-of-origin issues. This is only the beginning of an exciting journey
to recovery. Further exploration in this area is encouraged. The topics
provided thus far are meant only to broaden our horizons. As we continue

to gain insight into our disease of bulimia and our unhealthy concepts of self, we will find that we are replacing old behavior patterns with healthy behavior. With healthy behavior we can begin to love ourselves. As we love ourselves back to physical, emotional and spiritual health, we will find our world unfolding with each day of recovery.

18

Into Action

We have explored the disease of bulimia and its impact on our lives. Next we need a plan of action that will aid us in our recovery from the disease. It is useful to develop a plan that is simple and action oriented.

Recovery from bulimia and other addictions is a life-long process. That may sound depressing, but on the other hand, recovery is a very exciting experience with many new changes and life opportunities. For years we have lived in shame as bulimics, caught up and stuck in a vicious cycle of self-destructive behavior. Today we have choices about how we live our lives.

Available Support Systems

We can remain in our disease of bulimia or we can gather the courage it takes to tackle recovery and a new way of life. When we choose recovery, we need to decide first of all where we will go for support, information and aid. Many support systems are beginning to emerge in response to the needs of us with eating disorders. Some of these systems follow.

Self-Help Groups

American Anorexia/Bulimia Association, Inc.
133 Cedar Lane
Teaneck, New Jersey 07666
(201) 836-1800

National Association of Anorexia Nervosa
    and Associated Disorders
P. O. Box 7
Highland Park, Illinois 60035
(312) 831-3438

Overeaters Anonymous
P. O. Box 92870
Los Angeles, California 90009
(213) 542-8363

Self-help support groups operate on a national level and provide information about the different groups that meet all across the United States. They can be invaluable in providing the care and support that is so necessary for recovery from bulimia. As mentioned earlier, many of us have difficulty asking for help because it is a part of our disease. I encourage you to contact one of these groups or any local support groups in spite of whatever fear or shame you may experience in doing so.

Reaching Out For Support

It is important for us to begin reaching out to others. Many of us have tried for years in isolation, shame and loneliness to control our addiction to food, only to fail time and time again. When we find ourselves second guessing whether or not to call out for support and help from one of these groups, all we need to do is remember our past behavior at attempting to control our disease by ourselves.

Once we have made the decision to risk reaching out for support, it is crucial to follow through on this decision as soon as possible. We should set a target date and time for contacting support groups, such as within a week of making our decision to seek help.

Commitment To Seeking Help

Complete the following pledges.

** *My target date and time for loving myself enough to reach out to those support groups that will aid me in my recovery from bulimia are:*

Date: _____   Time: _____

Once I make this commitment, I promise myself that I will follow through with it.

** *After I have contacted those support groups that will aid me in my recovery from bulimia, I will commit to attending a group meeting within a week of my call.*

** *Now that I have contacted my support groups for the disease of bulimia, I am committed to attending my first group meeting on:*

Date: _____   Time: _____

** You have just made a far-reaching commitment to your recovery. **Congratulations!!!**

Supplementing An Existing Recovery Program

Some of us already are involved in support groups that are aiding us in our recovery from bulimia. We may be exploring this book in order to gain more insight into our disease. We may have discovered we need to add a different type of support group to our established recovery program. Possibly we have discovered that we need to find support groups that aid in addressing family-of-origin issues. Support groups that focus in on family-of-origin issues and further explore these areas are:

The National Association For Adult Children of Alcoholics
31582 Coast Highway, Suite B
Laguna Beach, California 92677
(714) 499-3889

Co-dependents Anonymous
Central Office
P.O. Box 5508
Glendale, Arizona 85312-5508
(602) 944-0141 (1-5 p.m.)

Next we will need to decide what issues in our life need our immediate attention. For most of us our first concern is our binging and purging behavior. We will need to develop a system in our program that will aid us in abstaining from binging behavior. Many of us purge through vomiting, laxative abuse, diuretic abuse, exercise and frequent dieting behavior. If any of these are a problem we will want to include them in our plan for abstinence.

Some of us may have used drugs or alcohol as a means of controlling our food addiction. If so, it is important to explore whether or not we need to address the issue of chemical addiction. This being the case, it is imperative that we address this issue with all the honesty we are capable of amassing. Like bulimia, the disease of chemical dependency is based on denial. If we are chemically addicted and this disease is not addressed, we will not be able to successfully recover from our bulimia. Chemical dependents not in recovery for that addiction are strongly encouraged to explore the many avenues of help available, such as Alcoholics Anonymous and Narcotics Anonymous, or to contact the local Council on Drugs and Alcohol.

It is useful to develop a plan of action that will aid us in our recovery process. Taking action means making a decision to take responsibility for who we are, doing something about our disease and following through to achieve recovery.

Sample Plans Of Action To Achieve Abstinence

A plan of action for working toward abstinence from binging and purging may be as follows:

Problem: Binging Behavior

How The Problem Is Identified

- Consuming large amounts of food in a short period of time
- Eating when not hungry
- Eating continuously

Goal: *Not binging*

Activities Which Will Facilitate Goal

- Keeping a food journal
- Going to support group meetings
- Telephoning group members when the urge to binge is present
- Eating three, complete, healthy meals per day
- Removing and abstaining from trigger foods that set off binging behavior

Problem: Purging Behavior

How The Problem Is Identified

- Vomiting
- Using laxatives
- Exercising excessively
- Using diuretics
- Not eating three meals a day

Goal: *Not purging*

Activities Which Will Facilitate Goal

- Keeping food journal
- Working with others in support group on healthy eating patterns
- Exercising no more than three times per week
- Removing all laxatives and diuretics from the house
- Calling support group members before purging
- Attending a minimum of three support groups per week

Other Issues Needing To Be Addressed

There also may be other issues we need to address that are interfering with our recovery and blocking our growth process. Examples of such issues are:

Problem: Isolating Behavior And Withdrawing From Others

How The Problem Is Identified:

- Isolating from support systems
- Difficulty in asking for help
- Not answering the door bell or telephone
- Not contacting friends or support systems when in pain

Goal: *Not isolating but reaching out to others*

Activities That Will Facilitate Goal:

- Attending support groups even during times of stress
- Making one telephone call per day to a support group member
- Sharing the urge to isolate with two support group members
- Experiencing feelings of anger, sadness, shame or pain

Problem: Handling Anger

How The Problem Is Identified:

- Difficulty in determining what anger feels like
- Questioning whether or not it is acceptable to feel anger
- Telling others not to be angry

- Making excuses for or covering up for others who have been abusive
- Discounting feelings of anger

Goal: *Being able to feel angry feelings*

Activities That Will Facilitate Goal:

- Becoming more aware of how the physical body reacts under stressful situations (eg, heart palpitations, headaches, high blood pressure, stomach problems and muscle tension, possible indicators of unexpressed anger)
- Recognizing feelings of irritation or sarcasm that may be hidden forms of anger
- Continuing to keep a food journal focusing on those eating behaviors that correlate with unexpressed anger
- Becoming more aware that the urge to binge may be about unexpressed anger
- Sharing angry feelings (when they are present) with two support group members for validation and reassurance

These are just a few examples of how we can begin addressing the issues that cause us difficulty. With a plan of action, not only have we defined the problem but also the action steps we need to take to begin resolving these issues.

Issues Needing Immediate Attention

Write out three issues you feel need your immediate attention in the format presented in the previous examples.

1. Problem:

How The Problem Is Identified:

Goal:

Activities That Will Facilitate Goal:

2. Problem:

    How The Problem Is Identified:

    Goal:

    Activities That Will Facilitate Goal:

3. Problem:

    How The Problem Is Identified:

    Goal:

    Activities That Will Facilitate Goal:

Conclusions

It is important for our recovery that we begin to love ourselves enough to spend the time and energy it takes to heal. In order for us to heal, we must start reaching out and allowing people who can be supportive, caring and reassuring to partcipate in our lives. Many of us have spent our lives being available to others and have never thought twice about lending a helping hand. Now, it is our turn to receive those who are willing to support us. We deserve the best life has to offer: love, friendship and peace of mind.

We can begin to share who we are with those who have suffered in the disease of addiction and despair as we have. Learning how to live life with the healthy tools we never had as childen and young adults becomes possible. We can begin to change those patterns of behavior we thought were ours for the rest of our lives. It becomes possible to develop new ways of thinking and being, which encourage physical, emotional and spiritual growth. As we begin to discover who we really are and what our potential is, we realize that we have some choices as to where our lives are going. For the first time, we can experience life and become a true participant in a world that has numerous avenues open for discovery.

We no longer have to avoid our feelings or escape the realities of life with addiction. We can continue to be confronted with difficult issues on a daily basis because now we have a set of tools that aid us in working through the many challenges of living. We try to live in the present, learning the lessons of life that each day has to offer. For the most part, life can become an exciting adventure. When we trip and fall down, the tools we have gained on our journey will seem to pick us up, brush us off and move us through whatever is needed to be experienced.

It is hopeful we all will be able to find the tools that will suit our recovery and move us from surviving life in shame to living life and evolving into the person we really want to be. These wishes don't have to remain dreams but can become realities with a little willingness and an open mind. Listen to that little inner spark of life that lives within and believes in each of you. **Give yourself the gift of recovery. You deserve it!**

Suggested Reading

Beattie, Melody, **Co-dependent No More**. Center City, MN: Hazelden Publishing, 1987.

Bradshaw, John. **Bradshaw On: The Family**. Deerfield Beach, FL: Health Communications, 1988.

_____ . **Healing The Shame That Binds You**. Deerfield Beach, FL: Health Communications, 1988.

Hollis, Judi. **Fat Is A Family Affair**. San Francisco, CA: Harper/Hazelden, 1986.

Kritsberg, Wayne. **Adult Children Of Alcoholics Syndrome**. Pompano Beach, FL: Health Communications, 1985.

Kübler-Ross, Elisabeth. **On Death And Dying**. New York, NY: MacMillan Publishing, 1969.

Millman, Marcia. **Such A Pretty Face**. New York: Berkley, 1981.

Norwood, Robin. **Women Who Love Too Much**. New York: Pocket Books, 1986.

Orbach, Susie. **Fat Is A Feminist Issue** and **Fat Is A Feminist Issue II**. New York: Berkley, 1978, 1982.

Palazzoli, M. **Self-Starvation**. New York: Aronson, 1978.

Phelps, J., and Norse, A. **The Hidden Addiction**. Boston: Little, Brown, 1986.

Polivy, J., and Herman, P. **Breaking The Diet Habit**. New York: Basic Books, 1983.

Schaef, A. W. **Co-Dependence: Misunderstood — Mistreated**. New York: Harper and Row, 1986.

Stuart, Mary S., and Orr, Lynnzy. **Otherwise Perfect**. Deerfield Beach, FL: Health Communications, 1988.

Subby, Robert. **Lost In The Shuffle, The Co-dependent Reality**. Pompano Beach, FL: Health Communications, 1987.

Woititz, Janet Geringer. **Adult Children Of Alcoholics**. Hollywood, FL: Health Communications, 1983.

Helpful 12-Step Books

HEALING A BROKEN HEART:
12 Steps of Recovery for Adult Children
Kathleen W.

This useful 12-Step book is presently the number one resource for all Adult Children support groups.

ISBN 0-932194-65-6 $7.95

12 STEPS TO SELF-PARENTING For Adult Children
Philip Oliver-Diaz and Patricia A. O'Gorman

This gentle 12-Step guide takes the reader from pain to healing and self-parenting, from anger to forgiveness, and from fear and despair to recovery.

ISBN 0-932194-68-0 $7.95

THE 12-STEP BOOKLETS
Mary M. McKee

Each beautifully illustrated booklet deals with a step, using a story from nature in parable form. The 12 booklets (one for each step) lead us to a better understanding of ourselves.

ISBN 1-55874-002-3 $8.95

UNDERSTANDING ME: Your Personal Story
Sharon Wegscheider-Cruse

This workbook shows the reader how to compile a three-generational family history and how to use the material to reshape the future.

ISBN 0-932194-29-X $13.95

GIFTS FOR PERSONAL GROWTH & RECOVERY
Wayne Kritsberg

A goldmine of positive techniques for recovery (affirmations, journal writing, visualizations, guided meditations, etc.), this book is indispensable for those seeking personal growth.

ISBN 0-932194-60-5 $6.95

Other Books By . . .

HEALTH COMMUNICATIONS, INC.

Enterprise Center
3201 Southwest 15th Street
Deerfield Beach, FL 33442
Phone: 800-851-9100

ADULT CHILDREN OF ALCOHOLICS
Janet Woititz
Over a year on The New York Times Best Seller list,this book is the primer
on Adult Children of Alcoholics.
ISBN 0-932194-15-X   **$6.95**

STRUGGLE FOR INTIMACY
Janet Woititz
Another best seller, this book gives insightful advice on learning to love
more fully.
ISBN 0-932194-25-7   **$6.95**

DAILY AFFIRMATIONS: For Adult Children of Alcoholics
Rokelle Lerner
These positive affirmations for every day of the year paint a mental picture
of your life as you choose it to be.
ISBN 0-932194-27-3   **$6.95**

*CHOICEMAKING: For Co-dependents, Adult Children and Spirituality
Seekers* — Sharon Wegscheider-Cruse
This useful book defines the problems and solves them in a positive way.
ISBN 0-932194-26-5   **$9.95**

LEARNING TO LOVE YOURSELF: Finding Your Self-Worth
Sharon Wegscheider-Cruse
"Self-worth is a choice, not a birthright", says the author as she shows us
how we can choose positive self-esteem.
ISBN 0-932194-39-7   **$7.95**

LET GO AND GROW: Recovery for Adult Children
Robert Ackerman
An in-depth study of the different characteristics of adult children of
alcoholics with guidelines for recovery.
ISBN 0-932194-51-6   **$8.95**

LOST IN THE SHUFFLE: The Co-dependent Reality
Robert Subby
A look at the unreal rules the co-dependent lives by and the way out of the
dis-eased reality.
ISBN 0-932194-45-1   **$8.95**

New Books . . .
from Health Communications

BRADSHAW ON: THE FAMILY: A Revolutionary Way of Self-Discovery
John Bradshaw
The host of the nationally televised series of the same name shows us how families can be healed and we as individuals can realize our full potential.
ISBN 0-932194-54-0 $9.95

HEALING THE CHILD WITHIN: Discovery and recovery for Adult Children of Dysfunctional Families — Charles Whitfield
Dr. Whitfield defines, describes and discovers how we can reach our Child Within to heal and nurture our woundedness.
ISBN 0-932194-40-0 $8.95

WHISKY'S SONG: An Explicit Story of Surviving in an Alcoholic Home
Mitzi Chandler
A beautiful but brutal story of growing up where violence and neglect are everyday occurrences conveys a positive message of survival and love.
ISBN 0-932194-42-7 $6.95

New Books on Spiritual Recovery . . .
from Health Communications

THE JOURNEY WITHIN: A Spiritual Path to Recovery
Ruth Fishel
This book will lead you from your dysfunctional beginnings to the place within where renewal occurs.
ISBN 0-932194-41-9 $8.95

LEARNING TO LIVE IN THE NOW: 6-Week Personal Plan To Recovery
Ruth Fishel
The author gently introduces you to the valuable healing tools of meditation, positive creative visualization and affirmations.
ISBN 0-932194-62-1 $7.95

GENESIS: Spirituality in Recovery for Co-dependents
by Julie D. Bowden and Herbert L. Gravitz
A self-help spiritual program for adult children of trauma, an in-depth look at "turning it over" and "letting go".
ISBN 0-932194-56-7 $6.95

GIFTS FOR PERSONAL GROWTH AND RECOVERY
Wayne Kritsberg
Gifts for healing which include journal writing, breathing, positioning and meditation.
ISBN 0-932194-60-5 $6.95

Books from . . .
Health Communications

THIRTY-TWO ELEPHANT REMINDERS: A Book of Healthy Rules
Mary M. McKee
Concise advice by 32 wise elephants whose wit and good humor will also
be appearing in a 12-step calendar and greeting cards.
ISBN 0-932194-59-1   **$3.95**

BREAKING THE CYCLE OF ADDICTION: For Adult Children of Alcoholics
Patricia O'Gorman and Philip Oliver-Diaz
For parents who were raised in addicted families, this guide teaches you
about Breaking the Cycle of Addiction from *your* parents to your children.
Must reading for any parent.
ISBN 0-932194-37-0   **$8.95**

AFTER THE TEARS: Reclaiming The Personal Losses of Childhood
Jane Middelton-Moz and Lorie Dwinnel
Your lost childhood must be grieved in order for you to recapture your
self-worth and enjoyment of life. This book will show you how.
ISBN 0-932194-36-2   **$7.95**

ADULT CHILDREN OF ALCOHOLICS SYNDROME: From Discovery to Recovery
Wayne Kritsberg
Through the Family Integration System and foundations for healing the
wounds of an alcoholic-influenced childhood are laid in this important
book.
ISBN 0-932194-30-3   **$7.95**

OTHERWISE PERFECT: People and Their Problems with Weight
Mary S. Stuart and Lynnzy Orr
This book deals with all the varieties of eating disorders, from anorexia to
obesity, and how to cope sensibly and successfully.
ISBN 0-932194-57-5   **$7.95**

Orders must be prepaid by check, money order, MasterCard or Visa.
Purchase orders from agencies accepted (attach P.O. documentation)
for billing. Net 30 days.

Minimum shipping/handling — $1.25 for orders less than $25. For
orders over $25, add 5% of total for shipping and handling. Florida
residents add 5% sales tax.